Interpersonal
Communication

An introduction to human interaction

Brent C. Oberg

MERIWETHER PUBLISHING LTD.
Colorado Springs, Colorado

Meriwether Publishing Ltd., Publisher
PO Box 7710
Colorado Springs, CO 80933-7710

Editor: Theodore O. Zapel
Assistant editor: Renée Congdon
Cover design: Jan Melvin

© Copyright MMIII Meriwether Publishing Ltd.
Printed in the United States of America
First Edition

Library of Congress Cataloging-in-Publication Data

Oberg, Brent C. (Brent Christopher)
  Interpersonal communication : an introduction to interpersonal communication / by Brent Oberg.
    v. cm.
    Contents: What is interpersonal communication and why should you care?
-- Making contact with others -- Listening skills -- Nonverbal
communication -- Managing conflict -- Persuasion -- Leadership skills --
Family communication -- Intercultural communication.
    ISBN 1-56608-085-1
1. Interpersonal communication. 2. Communication--Social aspects.
3. Social interaction. 4. Social perception. [1. Interpersonal
communication. 2. Communication.] I. Title.
    HM1166.O23 2003
    302.3'4--dc21
                            2003004807

1   2   3   4   03   04   05

Dedication

To my beautiful children,
Quinn, Soren, and Zoe
May the Lord bring as much joy to your lives
as you have brought to ours.

Contents

Chapter One

What Is Interpersonal Communication and Why Should You Care?

"I wonder what he really means by that."
"She said it, but I don't think she really meant it."
"You should have seen the look she shot me!"
"I hope I didn't say anything to offend him."
"You're a really good listener."
"She acts different when I'm alone with her than when she's in a large group."

If you've ever made statements like these, you are already a student of interpersonal communication. And who hasn't analyzed the communicative acts of themselves and those they encounter? It's only natural. After all, everyone communicates constantly. On a typical day, you may wake up and start the day by sharing breakfast with your family. At work or school, you probably spend much of your day listening to presentations, making calls, intermingling informally with friends, working in groups, attending meetings, meeting new people, and having discussions with others. If you spend the evening running errands, you encounter other shoppers and sales clerks. You may choose to go out to eat, where you interact not only with whomever you go with, but also waiters and perhaps other diners. Finally, you end your day at home, where you relate to your family, talk to friends on the phone, or send and receive emails.

Still, though we spend so much of our time interacting with others, often analyzing those interactions and sometimes having much to gain personally and professionally from our dealings with others, many of us know little of the process of communication and lack skills for communicating more effectively. Thus, the purpose of this book is to help you understand the underlying processes of interpersonal communication and to give you the knowledge and skills to become a more effective communicator.

The Relevance of Interpersonal Communication

There are numerous reasons to study interpersonal communication:

Interest

The field of interpersonal communication is fascinating, because it is really the study of what we do most of the time.

Self-Knowledge

Understanding how we communicate helps us understand ourselves better. In a way, the study of communication is the study of human nature. Communication theorist Stephen W. Littlejohn writes, "An understanding of systematic theories of communication is an important step toward becoming a more competent, adaptive individual" (4).

Health

The scientific evidence is overwhelming and undeniable: those who are connected to others are healthier. For instance, a 1995 article in *Newsweek* (Crowley, 62) demonstrates that social isolation is linked to stress, disease, and early death, while a study by T. R. Ruberman printed in the *Journal of the American Medical Association* (559-60) revealed that heart disease is more common among people who don't have strong interpersonal relationships.

Enjoyment

Almost everyone enjoys interacting with others. As J. Regis O'Connor says in his book *Speech: Exploring Communication,* "Whether face-to-face or over the telephone, good conversation can be one of life's most enjoyable pastimes" (13).

Personal Relationships

Communication skills help individuals develop more satisfying personal relationships. Common sense tells us that people who communicate well make more friends, have more dates, are more popular, and sustain friendships and marriages better than those who do not understand or practice the principles of effective communication. Studies confirm this. Conversely, we all know

2

people with poor communication skills. Maybe they are poor listeners, or they cannot maintain a conversation, or they talk about themselves too much. These are not individuals whose company we seek out or whom we choose as friends.

Professional Success

Communication is a key to success in almost every trade, occupation, and profession. In my speech classes, I challenge students to name a career that does not require communication skills. Invariably, they cannot do so. Tradespeople must be able to listen to their clients to satisfactorily meet their demands, salespeople must be able to persuade consumers to choose their product over a competitor's, managers must be able to offer clear direction and motivation to their employees. In *Communication Mosaics,* Julia T. Wood cites a survey in which 79 percent of New York City corporate executives ranked the ability to express ideas verbally as the most important qualification in hiring and evaluating employees (18).

Successful advertising executive Walter Gill once told me, "Business *is* presentation." He went on to explain how, in advertising, a multi-million dollar contract may hinge on one thirty-minute presentation. Those who are persuasive thrive; those who cannot communicate as well go out of business.

Civic Life

Wood says, "Citizens in a democracy must be able to express ideas and evaluate the ethical and logical strength of claims other people advance. To make informed judgments, voters need to listen critically to candidates' arguments and responses to questions" (18). This is not only true in the voting booth. As consumers, we must be able to listen to the claims of advertisers to discern fact from propaganda. When a product tells us they are recommended by three out of four doctors, we must wonder. Does this mean 75 percent of a large sample of doctors or literally three out of four? Are those doctors paid by the company which produces the product, or are they independent and devoid of bias?

A while back, a medicine advertised that its pills were "Little, yellow, different." A savvy consumer might justly ask questions. Is

3

little better? It may be easier to swallow, but it may also not have the strength of other remedies. What is inherently superior about a yellow capsule? Have you ever heard anyone say, "I'm feeling much better — that pill I took was yellow!" Finally, what is it different from? A weaker remedy? Medicine that actually works? A punch in the face? In our society, we are bombarded with messages. It is important that we understand how to listen to those messages so that we are not confused or misled.

You Cannot Not Communicate

Communication is so intrinsic to our lives it can be argued that it is impossible to not communicate. Say, for instance, that you are in line next to someone in the grocery store. You may choose to overtly communicate with that person, perhaps by smiling or saying hello. However, if you avoid eye contact or turn away from that person, you are telling them that you are closed to them, which tells much. Every move we make, every facial expression, even the clothing we wear communicates messages about ourselves. Not only is communication inevitable, it is also irreversible. Once a message is sent out, it cannot be called back.

Not that many of us try to avoid communication. The urge and the ability to communicate are innate. From the time babies are born, they communicate through their cries and thrive on attention and affection. Raymond Zeuschner of the California Polytechnic State University points out that Helen Keller, both blind and deaf, "set a dramatic example" (22). By learning to read and write, Keller affected countless individuals, achieving fame and widespread acclaim. But what if she'd never learned to read and write? Undoubtedly, none of us would have ever heard of her.

History of Communication Study

As long as people have existed, they have had a drive to connect and communicate with others. And almost as long as people have engaged in communication, they have sought to understand and improve their skills in this area. In 1799, the Rosetta Stone was discovered in Egypt. This stone, which was approximately 2,000 years old when it was discovered, was engraved with hieroglyphics. When those hieroglyphics were translated, it was discovered that part of them were actually a lesson in public speaking from the Egyptian Ptah-Hotep, who advised speakers to be clear, to address issues of concern to the listeners, and to have a strong delivery. Not bad advice.

Still, no society contributed more to the study of language and communication than that of Ancient Greece. About 2,600 years ago, the Greeks developed a city-state form of government in which citizens gathered in public meetings to debate matters of public policy. Because of this custom, the skills of public speaking and persuasion grew in importance. Thus, teachers of public speaking, called sophists, emerged. Originally, they were respected teachers, but eventually opportunistic sophists taught clever and tricky ways to persuade, and as a result the terms sophist and sophistry have negative connotations in our language today.

Many Greek scholars devoted themselves to the study of public speaking and communication. Socrates developed the method of teaching through questions and answers named the "Socratic Method" which is still widely used. Protagoras taught his students to carefully examine both sides of an issue before speaking in favor or in opposition to that subject. For this reason, he is known as the "father of debate." Perhaps the most important contributor to the study of communication in ancient Greece was Aristotle. Building on the ideas of Socrates and his teacher, Plato, Aristotle contributed ideas which are still widely accepted and studied today. Perhaps his most significant contribution to the study of rhetoric is his theory that for a message to be persuasive, it must have logic (logos), appeal to emotion (pathos), and derive from an ethical or trustworthy source (ethos).

Levels of Communication

Communication is defined as the process of sending and receiving messages to achieve understanding. Generally, the field of communication is broken down into different levels or settings:

Intrapersonal Communication
Intrapersonal communication is communication within

5

ourselves, or self-talk. When you think, daydream, solve problems, and imagine, you are practicing this form of communication.

Interpersonal Communication

As an interstate highway runs between two or more states, interpersonal communication is interaction that runs between two or more people. The basic level of interpersonal communication is a dyad, which describes one-on-one communication, but interpersonal communication can include communication among larger numbers of individuals as well. In order for an act of communication to be considered interpersonal, all participants must interact face to face and have the opportunity to mutually affect each other. A conversation, an interview, and a business dealing are all examples of this level of communication.

Small Group Communication

Work teams, social groups, decision-making committees, therapy groups, families, and groups of roommates are all small groups. The characteristics of small group communication are leadership, the sharing of ideas, peer pressure, specific roles for group members, norms and customs, and focus on a shared, group goal.

Public Communication

When you hear the term "communication," you may envision a speaker on stage behind a podium addressing an audience. Though the field of communication is actually much broader than such speeches, they do make up the area of public communication. It does not matter how large the audience is, public communication takes place whenever one person does most of the speaking while everyone else primarily serves as listeners.

Public communication is a very common and important level of communication. Teachers address their classes daily, students are often called upon to deliver speeches, lawyers address a courtroom, businesspeople speak at meetings, and candidates deliver speeches and debate in front of voters.

Organizational Communication

A more complex field, the study of what happens to messages as they travel around a large collection of individuals or groups who have a common goal is organizational communication. For instance, an organizational communication scholar may study the channels of communication within a university or a large corporation. This topic is very important as the effectiveness with which communication occurs within an organization can greatly affect productivity and even profits.

Mass Communication

There is much debate about the effect of media upon society. Do violent cartoons and movies make children more aggressive? Do advertisers perpetuate an unrealistic ideal of beauty by using young, thin models in commercials? Do television and film perpetuate racial stereotypes through their portrayal of minorities? Are teen suicides linked to rock music? These questions all relate to the study of mass communication.

Mass communication occurs when a message needs help to get from its source to its destination, there is usually some delay in sending and receiving, and feedback from the audience either does not occur or is considerably delayed. For instance, newscasters do not know who their messages reach or how effective they are until they see ratings and receive letters and calls from their viewers.

Intercultural Communication

Also called cross-cultural communication, this form of communication occurs between individuals of different cultural backgrounds. This setting for communication does not occur in isolation. Rather, intercultural communication is often present in all of the above levels of communication except, of course, intrapersonal. As the emphasis on multiculturalism and intercultural understanding and the globalization of business and media increases, this field becomes increasingly important.

Julia T. Wood of the University of North Carolina tells of a Taiwanese student who rarely spoke in class and would never participate in the heated debates that emerged in the classroom. Thinking that Mei-Ling lacked confidence, Wood encouraged her to speak up and argue for her ideas in class. Mei-Ling replied that doing so would be impolite because her culture considers it disrespectful to contradict others. Thus, a difference in cultural

7

background caused Wood to misunderstand her student (31).

The Communication Process

When communication takes place, there are six basic elements at work.

Source
The sender or originator of a message is the source.

Message
The message is the content or signal that the source sends to a receiver.

Receiver
The receiver is the listener or audience that interprets the message and then sends feedback to the source.

Channel
A channel is the sense — eyes, ears, nose, mouth, body — used to send the message. More than one sense can be used to send a message, and in fact, the accuracy with which the message is received increases when more channels are used. This is why face-to-face interaction is often more clear and powerful than a telephone conversation. On the telephone, you only hear the message. However, when you speak to someone in person, you also see their body language as they speak and respond to what you say.

Context
You don't speak the same way to a teacher or a boss as you would to your best friend. Likewise, you speak differently when at a basketball game or a concert than you might in church. This is because each of these are different contexts — the time, setting, and situation — in which communication occurs.

Noise
Anything that hinders or interferes with a message is called noise. There are three different types of noise. Perhaps you are distracted as you read this. You may be tired or have your mind on something else. Such thoughts and feelings are called psychological noise.

Physical noise consists of external distractions that occur when communication takes place in a noisy restaurant, or over blaring music, or on a loud and crowded street. Finally, when individuals have different meanings for symbols, like when a speaker uses a word not understood by the listener, semantic noise occurs.

Feedback

Feedback, the reactions of the listener to the source, may be verbal, nonverbal, or both. Listeners give feedback through comments, facial expressions, and body mannerisms. For instance, if your friend yawns, looks away, and fidgets as you speak, he may be telling you that he is bored with what you are saying.

Let's take a common situation: a teacher addressing a class. In this situation, the classroom, the time of day, and the subject being taught make up the communication context. The teacher is the source, the students are the receivers, and the lesson is the message. Many different channels of communication may be used as the instructor complements the verbal message with body language and writing on the chalkboard. Most likely, there is a great deal of noise. Students walking by the classroom, the view out the window, the hunger pains felt by the students waiting for lunch, and the students' daydreams about their dates for the weekend, the big game, or what they will have for lunch all cause distractions. Finally, the students send feedback to the instructor by asking questions, gazing out the window, looking confused, laughing, and taking notes.

A Model of Communication

A model is a visual representation of a process to help us understand it. We've all seen diagrams of football plays, with Xs for offensive players, Os for defensive players, and arrows to indicate where each player moves. Such diagrams are much easier to read and understand than would be a lengthy written description of the play. Likewise, theorists have created models to describe how the elements listed above interact to form the communication process. A basic model of communication follows:

9

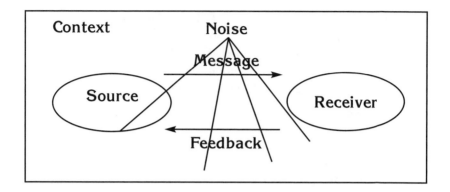

Conclusion

The field of communication is fascinating, and improved communication skills are of great benefit personally and professionally. Now that you understand how and why we communicate, we will move to specific areas of communication study. Whether you hope to become better at meeting others, listening, reading body language, resolving conflict, persuading others to your point of view, leading others, or relating better to individuals in other cultures or within your own home, knowledge of the communication process will help you.

Chapter Two

Making Contact with Others

Developing Self-Awareness and Self-Esteem

When we are young, our interactions grow outward from ourselves. Very young children are at first very self-centered, attending only to their own needs. Eventually they develop relationships with their parents and siblings, then extended family members, then larger and larger circles of friends and acquaintances.

Likewise, an understanding of how people communicate must grow outward from ourselves. To understand our interactions with others and to improve ourselves as communicators, we must first understand ourselves. More effective communicators tend to be self-aware. That is, they have a sense of their own individuality.

Self-concept is what you believe about yourself. It includes the attitudes, opinions, and beliefs you hold toward yourself. Your self-concept is based on many factors, including your body image, personal attributes and talents, values, and the social roles which you have chosen and which have been assigned to you. It is influenced not only by your interactions with others, but also the culture in which you live. For instance, the American media has a standard of beauty that few live up to; consequently, surveys repeatedly show that a high percentage of Americans are unhappy with the way they look.

When I was in high school, many of my friends told me how they couldn't wait to get to college where no one would know them or their reputation and they could meet new people with a "clean slate." I found it amusing when many of those individuals, upon arriving at college, did all they could to reinforce the personas they had in high school through their dress, conversation, and activities. The reason they did so is that people resist changing their self-concept. We grow comfortable with the way we see ourselves, which causes us to ignore messages that contradict our self-concept. For instance, if you see yourself as a bad singer, you will disregard a compliment about your voice as tact or a nicety. Also, like my friends, we often ritualize our behavior to maintain and reinforce our self-concept. For instance, someone who sees himself as a rebel will always dress against the norms of society and act aloof and brash.

Closely related to self-concept, self-esteem is the amount of satisfaction you have with yourself, or your own self-judgment. People with high self-esteem see themselves close to their vision of an ideal self while those with low self-esteem perceive themselves as inadequate, far from their ideal selves. Our interactions with others are greatly affected by our self-esteem. You probably know people who constantly put themselves down, saying things like "You're probably tired of talking to me," or "I better not go, I don't think anyone would really want me there." Such negativity is usually caused by low self-esteem. Ironically, bragging and self-absorbtion can also be the result of individuals trying to compensate for their low self-esteem. Most likely, you do not enjoy interacting with either of these types of individuals. Thus, more effective communicators tend to be individuals who think highly of themselves.

Communication Apprehension

Also called shyness or stage fright, communication apprehension is defined as an individual's level of fear or anxiety associated with either real or anticipated communication. While it is more problematic for some people than others, everyone suffers from communication apprehension. All of us have experienced nervousness before presenting a speech to an audience, interviewing for a job, meeting someone new, or asking that special someone for a date. Communication apprehension not only hurts our effectiveness as communicators, it's also no fun. Therefore, by understanding and controlling our nervousness, we can become more competent communicators and happier individuals.

Causes of Communication Apprehension

Communication apprehension can be either situational or

chronic. Chronic anxiety is not confined to specific situations. This is a more deep-seeded fear that is learned, much like a fear of heights, dogs, or crowds. Situational anxiety, on the other hand, is a response to a certain event or situation. Research has revealed five situational factors that can cause us to be unusually anxious when we communicate. First, we tend to become nervous when we are in the spotlight, which causes stage fright. This type of communication anxiety is so common that a 1973 study by R. H. Bruskin Associates found that the fear of public speaking was ranked as the number one fear among Americans, ahead of deep water, financial problems, height, insects, and even death (Work, 248).

Second, new situations cause increased anxiety. If you've never been to a job interview, you will feel more nervous than you would if you'd interviewed numerous times. Next, we tend to become nervous when interacting with people who are unfamiliar or whom we perceive as different, like someone from another country. Fourth, evaluation causes communication apprehension. A teacher may feel more nervous when being observed by an administrator than during a normal class period. The final situation that causes nervousness is past failure in a certain situation. If you have had a bad experience interacting with the opposite sex, for instance, you may be reticent to do so in the future.

Because we all, at one time or another, find ourselves in each of these situations, we all must deal with communication apprehension. So how do we do it? Below are some suggestions to help you cope with nervousness. Because the fear of speaking in public is so prevalent and is such a unique situation, it will be treated separately from the fear of dealing with people in more interpersonal situations.

Overcoming Stage Fright

Though communication apprehension can seem overwhelming before you give a speech or presentation, it is manageable and can actually be a good thing. Here are some suggestions to help you control your stage fright:

- **Realize the nervousness can help you.** Just as athletes try to turn their nerves into energy to help their performances, speakers can also use their anxiety to get "pumped up." When you're nervous, your energy level increases. This can translate into increased enthusiasm in your speech. Take that energy and do something positive with it. Move around, use gestures, and speak with variety and inflection.

- **Be prepared.** Since most stage fright comes from a fear of failure, you can decrease your nerves by increasing your level of preparedness. It's like taking a test. Sure, you may always be nervous when a teacher or professor gives a test, but aren't you a lot less worried when you've studied for the test and feel you know the material inside and out? The same is true of speaking. You may always be nervous before a presentation, but time spent writing and practicing the speech will yield greater confidence.

- **Choose a topic in which you strongly believe.** If you are passionate about your speech, you will focus less on your nerves and more on the content of your speech. I once had a student in speech class whose fear of speaking was so great he usually refused to speak. However, when it came time to do demonstration speeches, he was actually excited to speak. Why? Because he had chosen to do a speech on his passion: snowboarding. If he had selected topics that elicited such excitement for the other assignments, he would have done well in the class.

- **Realize the audience is on your side.** Your audience understands what you are going through. Most of them have had to make speeches before and empathize with your stage fright.

- **Don't be afraid to make mistakes.** Because your audience is sympathetic, they will forgive mistakes. Besides, mistakes are inevitable. In conversation, we constantly stumble over words, stutter, and pause for a second while we think of the right thing to say. Such disfluencies rarely disrupt an informal discussion, so why would they ruin a speech? Further, all

14

mistakes seem magnified to the speaker. If you maintain your composure, chances are the audience may not even notice a mistake that, to you, seems crucial.

- **Practice relaxation techniques.** Walk before you present, take deep breaths, dangle your arms and twirl your wrists, make yourself yawn. Such techniques will help reduce the physical symptoms of stage fright, which will make you feel less nervous.

- **Use positive visualization.** Before you speak, close your eyes and imagine yourself presenting your speech perfectly. Imagine yourself speaking with charisma and energy while using movement, gestures, and facial expressions to enhance the performance. Picture the audience listening intently and responding positively to your presentation. This confidence-building technique is used effectively by many types of performers, including athletes.

- **Use humor in your speech.** Not only will humor make your speech more interesting and help hold the attention of the audience, it can also help you (and your audience) relax. How? Humor builds rapport between the speaker and the audience and elicits a response, laughter, that gives the speaker confidence. A successful joke, especially near the beginning of the speech, can give the speaker a real boost.

- **Focus on your speech.** Stage fright occurs when the speaker focuses more on the experience of speaking and the nerves caused by that experience than the matter at hand. In the movie *Carbine Williams*, the title character, played by Jimmy Stewart, explains how he survived solitary confinement while in prison. He points out that it is impossible to think of two things at once. Therefore, while confined, he kept his mind off his pain by thinking about more pleasant topics. Likewise, rather than dwelling on your stage fright, focus on what you plan to say.

- **Practice speaking as much as possible.** With practice,

15

almost everything becomes easier. Stage fright does drastically decrease with speaking experience. Of course, those who suffer from communication apprehension usually avoid situations in which they will be asked to speak. Don't do this. Take every opportunity you have to address an audience, no matter how unpleasant it may seem at first, and you will find that public speaking will become easier. Who knows? You may grow to enjoy it!

What Is Shyness?

Shyness is a nearly universal human trait. Everyone has moments when they feel shy, and according to *U.S. News and World Report*, about half of those surveyed consider themselves shy while roughly one out of every eight people are so timid that interactions with other people are a source of dread (Schrof and Schultz). Many famous and accomplished people have suffered from this form of communication anxiety, including Eleanor Roosevelt, Robert Frost, and Albert Einstein.

There are those who believe that this problem is growing as our culture increasingly isolates us from each other. The internet, ATM machines, pay-at-the-pump gas stations, and grocery stores that allow you to check yourself out all decrease the amount of face-to-face interaction in which we engage. As Lynne Henderson, a Stanford University researcher and director of the Shyness Clinic in Menlo Park, California, says, "If people were slightly shy to begin with, they can now interact less and less. And that will make the shyness much worse." It almost sounds like a bad joke, but the same *U.S. News* article tells how, at one social phobia information session at the Shyness Clinic, only one man showed up. All the others who were supposed to attend were too shy to come (Schrof and Schultz).

Research has shown that more women than men suffer from social anxiety. For instance, a study by Marjorie A. Jaasma, an Assistant Professor of Communication at California State University at Stanislaus, found that female students have higher communication apprehension in the context of a college classroom and that females see that arena as one in which they are

16

conspicuous and are judged by both their instructors and their peers. However, men seek professional help for shyness more often, probably because shyness and demureness are considered more favorable traits in women than in men (219-28).

The cost of shyness is also high. Research reveals that being shy cannot only create loneliness, but can also cause health problems and lower your earning potential. So it is important that we are able to identify the causes and signs of shyness and learn techniques to help us overcome our social anxiety.

You Are Shy If...
- You become very nervous when meeting new people.
- You lack confidence when interacting with others.
- You want to talk to more people, but are still unable to do so.
- You become tense if you try to initiate a conversation.
- You spend far more time alone than you would like.
- You are especially nervous talking to someone you would like to date.
- You often replay entire conversations in your mind, regretting what you said or wishing you had said something different.
- Others see you as very quiet.

Perhaps the most difficult situation for shy people is meeting someone new. There are three reasons we fear strangers. First, outmoded nineteenth century social restrictions that mandated that strangers should be introduced by a third party before beginning a conversation still resonate and affect our behavior. Many people believe it "wouldn't be proper" to introduce themselves to a stranger. Also, when we are young, we are taught never to talk to strangers. While practical and necessary advice for children, this can create lifelong fear. Finally, negative self-talk can cause us to fear strangers. If you frequently tell yourself that others don't want to talk to you or often regret things you say, you begin to believe your internal dialog and see yourself as inferior or unworthy.

Overcoming Shyness
So, you're thinking, I know what shyness is. Give me something that will help! If you suffer from chronic shyness, you

may need to seek professional help. But for most of us, knowing a few strategies and coping techniques can help reduce social anxiety and shyness:

- **Use affirming self-talk.** It only stands to reason: if negative self-talk helps create shyness, a positive internal dialog can help cure it. According to psychologist Nancy Wesson, Ph.D, we should replace negative thoughts with affirmations like, "I can learn to overcome my shyness," "I can make mistakes when talking to new people and still pursue a relationship," and "I can become comfortable talking in meetings." Also, if rejection causes you to label yourself as "lame" or "stupid," you must realize that such labels are not only harmful, they are also untrue.

- **Use relaxation techniques.** The techniques described earlier can help you relax before an interpersonal interaction just as they can before a speech.

- **Have an outward, rather than an inward, focus.** When conversing, focus on the other person and what they are saying. Do not rehearse what you will say next or dwell on your nerves or awkwardness while someone else is speaking.

- **Use an effective icebreaker.** No, I'm not talking about cheesy pick-up lines like, "Do you believe in love at first sight or do I have to walk past you a second time?" An icebreaker is an opening statement that can effectively begin a conversation with anyone, not just prospective dates. Perhaps the best icebreaker is one that comments on a shared experience with the person you hope to meet. For instance, if you are in a class with someone, you might say, "This is the most boring class I've ever been in. How about you?" Other effective ways to open a conversation include asking for information ("Do you know what our assignment was?"), giving a compliment ("That's a great shirt!"), or using humor ("By the time they get around to helping us, we'll be ready to retire!").

18

- **Reframe rejection.** When others decline an offer from you, don't try to read their minds. Don't assume that they turned you down because they don't like you or because you are inadequate or socially inept. There could be hundreds of reasons for their refusal. Say, for instance, you ask a coworker to have lunch with you. That person responds, "I'm swamped today — maybe some other time." You may assume that individual doesn't like you, but it is possible that she was telling truth and would really love to have lunch with you if she wasn't so busy. If you frame rejection as a refusal of you, your self-esteem will be damaged and you may become even more shy. However, if you avoid making assumptions based on facts not in evidence, you will have a more positive — and realistic — interpretation of rejection.

- **Plan to be rejected.** Let's get real: there are people who will spurn overtures from you and people who will not like you. But to have meaningful relationships and rewarding interactions, you must risk, and sometimes deal with, rejection. Just remember: people who will not like you are probably in the minority and the rewards of risk taking are far greater than the pain of rejection. After all, if you choose to begin a conversation with someone, it is probably because you recognize that you have something in common. It is reasonable to assume, then, that they will enjoy interacting with you for the same reason.

Conversation Skills

While it may be difficult to make contact with other people, it can be just as difficult to interact with them once you've met them. In fact, very few of us are very good conversationalists. Too often, we talk about ourselves, don't listen effectively, and remain closed to those with whom we converse. Thus, everyone can benefit by understanding basic conversational principles.

Asking Questions

One of my friends is an outstanding conversationalist because he asks others questions, which involves everyone in discussion by getting them to talk about themselves and their areas of interest. There are two types of questions. Ritual questions, primarily used at the beginning of a conversation, focus on people's names, where they are from, and what they do. Informational questions are more specific, designed to elicit information about other people's ideas, beliefs, and experiences. To be a good conversationalist, you must not only be able to ask ritual questions, you must be able to ask informational questions about topics important to the other person. Have you ever met a person who seemed very quiet, until you got them talking about something important to them, and then you wondered if they would ever stop talking? You simply asked an effective informational question. And, since we all have issues or experiences we love to discuss, anyone can be engaged in conversation.

How do you know what type of questions to ask of others? If you have any prior knowledge of them, you can use that. For instance, if you've been told that someone is an avid golfer, you could ask them if they had any good rounds lately. Or, if someone is wearing a T-shirt advertising a bike race, ask if they participated in that race or if they enjoy bicycling. If you don't know anything about your partner in conversation, then you must ask follow-up questions based on the responses you receive to the questions you have already asked. To do this, you must practice active listening.

Active Listening

To be an effective conversationalist, you must also practice the principles of active listening, which are described in greater depth in Chapter Three of this book. My friend is not a good conversationalist just because he asks questions. He also genuinely cares about the responses to those questions. Active listening involves carefully attending to what the other person is saying, rephrasing what the other person has said to let that individual know they have been heard, and providing feedback to the speaker.

Self-Disclosure

The third component of conversation is self-disclosure, the revelation of personal information. Whenever we tell someone something about ourselves they wouldn't otherwise know, such as personal thoughts, feelings, and experiences, self-disclosure occurs. Simply, intimacy cannot occur without self-disclosure. Common sense tells us that we can never grow close to those with whom we are unwilling to share anything more than simple, factual information. Further, self-disclosure breeds self-disclosure. Have you ever been afraid to say something personal until your partner in conversation did so? Most likely, you forgot your inhibitions and felt more comfortable sharing. In fact, research has found that self-disclosure is both a means of developing closeness with others as well as a gauge of intimacy in a relationship.

Not only does self-disclosure help develop intimacy, it also makes you healthier. Have you ever felt that you "couldn't wait" to tell someone your good news or just had to get something "off your chest." This is because, as humans, we have a need to share information about ourselves. Sidney Jourard, a social philosopher and clinical psychologist, observed that his patients tended to become closed to the world, but grew healthier when they disclosed themselves to a therapist.

The Johari Window

The Johari Window provides a helpful model to help us understand self-disclosure. Developed in the 1960s by Joseph Luft and Harry Ingham, this diagram represents how much we know about ourselves and how much others know about us. Four possible combinations of knowledge about the self are illustrated: (1) information you and others know about you, (2) information you know about yourself that no one else knows, (3) information others know about you that you do not know, and (4) information about you not known by yourself or others. These four types of knowledge are divided into quadrants, causing the diagram to look like a window with four panes of glass. This trait, along with a combination of the first names of the creators of this diagram, give the Johari Window its name.

The quadrant representing information about you known to all is called the **open pane**. This includes knowledge of your physical appearance, gender, and occupation. The **hidden pane** represents the knowledge you have about yourself that is concealed from others, such as private dreams and fantasies or an aspect of your past you wish to keep secret. This is the information you conceal even from those closest to you. The things others know about you that you are unaware of is illustrated by the **blind pane**. This is information you are unable, or unwilling, to recognize. You might have a friend who mistakenly thinks he's a great dancer. At parties, he always goes to the middle of the dance floor and flails about awkwardly. Even though everyone laughs about his lack of prowess on the dance floor, no one has the heart to tell him that he can't dance. Thus, the fact that he is a terrible dancer is in your friend's blind pane. Finally, there is information about you that no one has yet discovered. This information makes up the unknown pane. For instance, I never knew that I was allergic to cats until, in college, I stayed with a friend who had a cat. Until I suffered through that night, my allergy was unknown to me and everyone else.

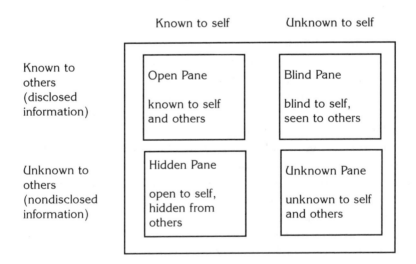

Since all of us disclose different amounts of information to others, a Johari Window representing each of us would look different as our panes vary in size. A very private person, for instance, may have large hidden panes and smaller open panes. So how can this help us improve our skills as conversationalists? It helps us understand ourselves, which is foundational to understanding others. It is important to gain access to our unknown areas so that we can see what others see in us and even learn things about ourselves no one knows. Also, if others seem closed to us, we can help them learn to open up and gain access to that information.

Opening Up: Practicing Self-Disclosure

Since self-disclosure satisfies a natural drive, develops intimacy, and builds health, you want to open yourself to others. But how? First, you must be willing to take the risk of sharing personal information. However, you do not want to do so too abruptly or quickly. I'm sure you've encountered someone who told you intimate details of their past or private life just a few minutes after you first met. Most likely, this turned you off as you wondered, "Who is this person and why are they telling me this?" Normally, we only reveal superficial information at the beginning of a relationship and gradually work our way to more intimate disclosures. In order for this dynamic to continue, however, reciprocity is important. If you disclose personal information to someone and they don't reciprocate, you are unlikely to disclose anything further. Likewise, if you hope to continue developing intimacy in a relationship, you must return the disclosures of the other person with your own revelations.

Other Conversation Skills

In addition to these basic principles, some suggestions, hints, and reminders can also help you improve your conversational skills:

- **Remember people's names.** Make a conscious effort to hear and remember the names of others when you are introduced to them. I know I'm bad at this. Too often, when someone tells me their name, it goes in one ear and out the other. One trick to help you remember other people's names is to use them in conversation. For instance, don't ask, "What do you do?" when you could ask, "What do you do, James?" You'll notice that people in professions that require them to remember large numbers of names, like the clergy, do this. Word association can also help you remember names. When you first meet someone, link their name to a visual picture conjured by their name.

- **Build rapport.** To help you connect with others, look for things you have in common. Mutual acquaintances, common experiences, or similar likes and dislikes can all help you start and maintain a conversation. For instance, if someone is wearing a T-shirt advertising an NFL team, ask if they think their team has a chance at the Superbowl this year. If you are vacationing in the same place, ask if they've seen any sights they would recommend to you.

- **Recall your last conversation.** Others will be flattered if you remember things they have told you in the past. For instance, if someone mentioned that they were preparing for a big test the last time you talked, ask them how it went when you see them next. This also serves the purpose of letting others know you are truly interested in what they have to say.

Interviewing

One specific type of interpersonal communication that is particularly crucial is the interview. An exchange of questions and answers, an interview has the potential to change your life. When you hear this term, you most likely think of a job interview, but there are actually numerous types of interviews:

Information-Giving Interviews

Often, this type of interview occurs between a person who is new to a situation and someone who is an expert and has information to help the novice become acquainted. Though the expert may structure the interaction, the new person will probably ask most of the questions. For instance, someone new to a job may work with an experienced employee until they are ready to work independently. Doctors explaining to patients how to take

24

medicines or how to recognize symptoms, or academic advisors explaining curricular requirements to students, are also examples of information-giving interviews.

Information-Gathering Interviews

Public opinion polls, census taking, research surveys, and journalists' interviews of subjects are all examples of this type of interview. An information-gathering interview may be used any time you are trying to learn information from an expert in a particular field. Unlike information-giving interviews, the interviewer usually structures the communication in this type of interview.

Persuasive Interviews

Interviews designed to influence attitudes or actions, like a sales pitch, are persuasive interviews. Chances are, if you've ever visited a car dealer, you have experienced this communication situation as the salesperson asked questions like, "Is safety important to you?" and "What can I do to put you in a car today?"

Problem-Solving Interviews

If you ever sought out a teacher or professor to help you improve your performance in a class, or if you discussed a problem in the workplace with a coworker or supervisor, you have participated in a problem-solving interview.

Counseling Interviews

When you seek help with a personal problem, you are initiating a counseling interview. Most notably, sessions with psychologists or professional counselors fall into this category, as do meetings with attorneys for legal advice and discussions with accountants regarding financial issues.

Complaint Interviews

Complaint interviews allow people to express dissatisfaction with a product, service, or person. When you call a company's customer service line to complain, your discussion with the representative falls into this category.

Appraisal Interviews

Many employers conduct regular performance reviews, in which supervisors meet with employees to discuss the worker's achievements and strengths as well as their weaknesses, problems, and goals for professional development. Such discussions are appraisal interviews.

Selection Interviews

Any interview in which individuals are screened for hire, awards, advancement, or placement is a selection interview. The most notable of these interviews is the job interview, because of the ramifications. When you interview with a prospective employer, much is at stake: perhaps your dream job and significant amounts of money. Because of the importance of this type of interview, many of us grow very nervous and struggle to say the right things. Conducting a job interview is not easy, either. You have to be able to ask questions that are not only legal and ethical, but will also help you find the right person for the job you need to fill. For this reason, suggestions for interviewing and being interviewed are provided here.

Getting the Job — Being Interviewed

Unless you are independently wealthy or have recently won a huge lotto jackpot, you will almost certainly interview for a job at some point in your life. In fact, most people are interviewed dozens of times.

Unfortunately, employees are not always hired on their ability in their chosen field. That is not readily apparent to employers. Rather, the job interview usually determines who will get the job — and the salary, benefits, and opportunities that go along with it — and who must continue to look for work. Therefore, knowing how to successfully interview with prospective employers can be of great value.

- **Practice before you go to the interview.** Have a friend or family member act as the employer and ask you questions they think you might face in the actual interview. Then pay close attention to any suggestions they offer. This will decrease your nerves, give you time to think of responses to possible questions, and provide you with feedback on your interviewing technique.

- **Take a number of copies of your resume with you.** Take at least one resume for each person who is on the interview team. If you don't know how many people will be conducting the interview, take four or five copies. Be sure your resume is neat and professional and that it lists your abilities and accomplishments, casting you in the best possible light. If you don't know how to write a resume, help is readily available. There are countless books on the subject as well as computer programs that provide preset formats for resumes. You may also ask friends who are experienced job hunters for copies of their resumes to use as examples.

- **Be sure all spelling, grammar, and punctuation is correct in your resume and other materials.** Once, while on a team considering applicants to teach English at our school, I came across a resume with a handful of words misspelled and a punctuation error. Needless to say, this applicant was immediately disqualified from consideration. Also, make sure all writing is gender neutral. Ann Humphries, founder and president of ETICON, Inc. and a consultant to several Fortune 500 companies, notes that some mail addressed to her by potential applicants will say, "Dear Sir." Not only is such phrasing outdated, it is often (as in the case of mail received by Humphries) inaccurate. If you can address a letter specifically to an individual, use that person's name. Otherwise, address mail "To Whom It May Concern," or "Dear Human Resources Manager." Check the spelling of the name of the company a number of times. Most companies won't hire someone who can't even spell their name correctly!

- **Take other personal artifacts.** If you have any other materials that show your proficiency in a field, take them to the interview as well. For instance, if you are applying for a job as a newspaper reporter, take some of your best stories from your last job in journalism or even writings for your high school or college paper. Anything that shows your ability can help you get hired.

- **Dress professionally.** Once, my wife competed for a job with one other applicant. My wife was surprised to see the other applicant leave her job interview in shorts, sandals, and a casual shirt. My wife, on the other hand, wore the most professional business suit she owned. Guess who got the job? Always, always, always dress your best for an interview. Otherwise, you may tell your prospective employer that you are unprofessional or that you don't care about this job before you even say a word.

- **Do your homework.** Find out as much about your prospective employer as you can before you go to the interview by looking at their website or a business directory at the library. If they ask, "Why do you want to work for us?" you should be able to say more than, "I dunno, I was hoping you would pay me money." Learn the strengths and weaknesses of the organization with which you are seeking employment and work these into the interview. Also, if you can find out the names of any individuals you will encounter at your interview, learn them before you leave and use them when you talk to those people at your interview.

- **Be on time.** If necessary, drive to the location of the interview in advance so you won't get lost on your way. Leave early to account for any unexpected problems, such as a traffic jam. If you're late to the interview, the employer will assume you may often be late to work.

- **Be positive.** Don't look at the interview as an interrogation. Instead, consider it a chance to brag a little. I mean, how often do you get to talk about your virtues in great depth? Most of your friends would be bored if you went on about your talents and abilities the way you are expected to in an interview. Show your positive attitude through your manner. Shake hands with vigor, walk with confidence, smile at everyone you meet, maintain eye contact while listening and speaking, sit up straight, and avoid any nervous fidgeting.

- **Elevate your language.** Ann Humphries says, "Profanity is out of course. But also watch for colloquialisms in your speech — 'yep,' 'nope,' 'no problem.' Don't ramble. Watch out for nervous humor. Don't preface a question with, 'May I ask you a question?' "

- **Answer questions directly.** Don't skirt an issue or answer a question you wish had been asked instead of the one that really was.

- **Be complete.** Never give a one-word response to a question. For example, if the interviewer asks if you have any experience in this field, don't say, "yes," and then wait for the next question. Elaborate and describe the experience you do have. If you have a chance, work in information you want them to know. When they ask if you have experience, you may tell how you not only worked in another retail situation, for instance, but also set the record for total sales in a month at your old store.

- **But be concise.** While responses must be complete, they should not be overly long. Keep your examples and stories short and to the point. If you are a bore in an interview, it will be assumed you will be a bore as a coworker.

- **Engage in person-centered communication.** Think of the needs and wants of the person interviewing you. If you were in their shoes, what would you want in an applicant? Help them to see that you are the person who can meet their needs.

- **Be prepared for behavioral interviewing.** According to Seattle career counselor, national speaker, and author Robin Ryan, many employers are now using this type of interview, which gives applicants very specific examples of positive and negative work scenarios to determine exactly how they would handle pressure and respond to difficult situations. Examples of behavioral questions include, "Tell me about a time you've dealt with a difficult customer. How did you respond?" or "A student swears at you in class. What do you do?" To successfully handle behavioral questions, Ryan suggests you prepare for this type of question: keep your responses short and to the point and provide examples of instances in the past when you've successfully dealt with similar situations.

- **Ask for the job.** Make it clear that you want the job. Employers want someone who wants to work for them. Also, ask for follow-up. It is entirely appropriate to ask when a decision might be made or when you'll next be contacted.

- **Send a thank-you note.** Very soon after the interview, write a letter or an email thanking the interviewers for their time and consideration. This not only shows that you know etiquette, it also keeps your name in their minds as they consider other applicants and make their decision.

Interviewing Others

Though it may not be as nerveracking as interviewing for a job, interviewing others can also be difficult and is a very important skill. Just as an applicant has very little time to impress a potential employer, the employer has precious little time to choose the best person for a job. Though you may not realize it now, you will most likely interview others for employment. Modern interviewing strategies often emphasize interviewing teams as opposed to leaving the selection process up to one individual, such as the CEO or the director of personnel. You will certainly interview others for various other reasons, such as research for an assignment. When you do, consider the following:

- **Be prepared.** Know something about the person you are interviewing. In an employment interview, read the applicant's resume and cover letter carefully, committing important information to memory. In other types of interviews, do as much research on your subject as possible. Also, have a list of questions you want to ask ready.

- **Be an active listener.** Make eye contact with the interviewee, provide verbal and nonverbal feedback, and be interested in what they have to say. You will want to take careful and complete notes of the interview so you can remember what the respondent said, but you must do so quickly so you can resume listening.

- **Keep an open mind.** Especially when interviewing applicants for employment, you must place any prejudices aside. You may lose out on an outstanding employee if they hold an opinion that you disagree with or a style of dress against the applicant.

- **Avoid illegal questions.** It is illegal for a potential employer to ask for information that is intrusive and irrelevant to job qualifications, including questions about race, ethnicity, marital status, age, political affiliation, and disability. To stay within the law and to run an ethical interview, you must be aware of and abide by these regulations.

Assertiveness

Many people today benefit from assertiveness training, which teaches individuals to express their feelings and to defend their legitimate rights without violating the rights of others. It is important to note that assertiveness is not aggressiveness as it considers the needs of others and is far more effective in achieving interpersonal objectives.

No one is constantly assertive. You may have no trouble being assertive with your family but might not be able to do so with strangers or your boss. As Matthew McKay, Martha Davis, and Patrick Fanning point out in their book *Messages: The Communication Skills Book*, this is why everyone can benefit from an introduction to these principles. They say, "Assertiveness training can expand the number of social situations in which you can respond assertively rather than passively or aggressively" (113).

The Three Basic Styles of Communication

According to McKay, Davis, and Fanning, humans have three basic styles of communicating: assertively, aggressively, and passively. The first step in assertiveness training is learning to identify each style (115-18).

The Passive Style

Individuals who use the passive style of communication don't directly express their thoughts, feelings, and desires. They may either subjugate their feelings entirely or try to communicate in more subtle ways, like frowning, crying, or whispering under their breath. Passive communicators typically use a soft, uncertain voice and often make disclaimers before they speak, such as "I'm no expert," or "I'm not really sure, but ... " In short, those who use the passive style rarely get what they want because they keep their desires to themselves.

The Aggressive Style

On the other hand, those who communicate with the aggressive style have no trouble telling others what they want. The problem is how they do it. Aggressive communicators assert their own desires and wishes in a way that violates the rights and feelings of others. Aggressive communicators use sarcasm or put-downs to humiliate and embarrass others, often go on the attack when they don't get their way, and have an air of superiority. Physically, they behave in an intimidating manner, often pointing or gesticulating with a closed fist and maintaining a stiff and rigid posture. Though aggressive communicators are able to state their feelings, they are inevitably ineffective as they turn others against them.

The Assertive Style

People who communicate assertively are able to confirm both themselves and others as they make direct statements about their wants, feelings, and wishes, but do so in a way that takes into account the rights and feelings of others. Assertive communicators clearly and directly state what they want in a respectful, nonjudgmental manner. Physically relaxed and self-assured, assertive individuals listen carefully, let others know they have been heard, make direct requests and refusals, and are open to compromise so long as it isn't at the expense of their own rights. The assertive style is a very effective style of communication because it takes everyone into account.

Perhaps the three styles of communication can best be understood through examples of how each type of communicator would express the same message:

Passive	Aggressive	Assertive
If you don't want to have dinner with me, that's OK.	I demand we go have dinner tonight.	I would very much like dinner with you tonight.
If you want me to make the presentation, I'll do it.	I don't care what you need, there is no way you're getting me to speak at this meeting.	I am not prepared to speak on this issue. I have to say no.
It would be nice to have this report today, but if you don't have time, I suppose it can wait.	This must be done today,so I hope you can work faster than last time.	It is important that this is done today. Can you do that for me?

How to Communicate Assertively

According to McKay, Davis, and Fanning, an assertive statement has three parts (120):

1. Your perspective of the situation.
2. Your feelings about the situation.
3. Your wants regarding the situation.

To communicate assertively, you must avoid blaming or labeling others. When you state your perspective of the situation, try to do so in objective terms. For instance, an assertive student who has a problem with a teacher might confront the problem by saying, "I was disappointed in my grade on the research paper. It seems as though you have different standards for me than the rest of the class, which makes me feel like I can't succeed. Would you please go over my paper with me and explain what I need to do to get a higher grade next time?"

Listening is also an important part of assertive communication. As with speaking, assertive listening also has three parts:

1. Prepare to listen by eliminating distractions and making sure you are mentally tuned in.
2. Listen. Fully devote your attention to the other person. Try to read their feelings and hear what they want. If you need

33

the speaker to clarify or give you more information, ask questions.
3. Acknowledge that you heard the other person by paraphrasing what they have said and, if appropriate, empathizing with their feelings.

Special Assertive Techniques

You may be thinking that assertive communication sounds easy when you're reading about it, but implementing it in interpersonal interactions is another story. You're right. To help you remain assertive at the most difficult times — when someone is criticizing you, when you are angry, or when the other person is not receptive to your approach — it is helpful to have a few specific assertive techniques at the ready.

The Broken Record Technique

When dealing with someone who just doesn't seem to "get it," the broken record technique is especially helpful. With this technique, you acknowledge the other person's feelings and concerns, but continue to repeat a short, specific, easy to understand statement about what you want until the listener realizes that you mean what you say. This technique can be used in a variety of situations, and is best applied in situations where you are unwilling to compromise. Educational theorists Lee and Marlene Canter note that the broken record technique is especially helpful for parents dealing with children or teachers dealing with difficult parents (212). An example of how you might use the broken record technique with a door-to-door salesperson follows:

Salesperson: I would like to show you this marvelous new vacuum that I am sure you will want to purchase.
Customer: I never buy from door-to-door salespeople. Thank you.
Salesperson: But if you take the time to watch my demonstration, I'm sure you'll change your mind.
Customer: I am sure your demonstration is impressive and that you have a fine product, but I never buy from door-to-door salespeople.

Salesperson: But this vacuum has so many features. If you ...

Customer: I appreciate the features, but my policy remains the same. I do not buy from door-to-door salespeople. Now please excuse me.

Salesperson: OK, OK. Thank you for your time.

Content-to-Process Shift

When you feel that the focus of a conversation has drifted from what you want to talk about or when a discussion is becoming too heated, it is often helpful to use a content-to-process shift. With this technique, you simply move the conversation away from the content, or the issue at hand, to what is going on between you and the other person. For instance, if a conversation becomes intense, you might say, "I feel we are both losing our tempers. This is an emotional issue for both of us, but we'll never get anything done if we don't discuss it rationally." If you can comment on the process of communication in an unbiased, objective tone, you may be able to refocus the conversation on the issue at hand.

Momentary Delay

Rather than blurting out something you might later regret, it is often a good idea to take a moment to analyze what has been said, restrain your emotions, and choose your response carefully. An added benefit of using a momentary delay is that it also gives the other person time to regain composure and to think as well.

Time Out

If your parents gave you time outs when you were young, this phrase may carry a negative connotation for you. However, when a discussion of an important issue becomes much too heated, it can be helpful to take a break until both parties have an opportunity to cool down. It is important when you use this technique, however, that you set a time in the near future to meet and resume the discussion. A time out should not be a way to avoid resolving an issue.

Conclusion

Meeting and interacting with other people can at times be difficult, but it is also extremely rewarding. In fact, it is vital to our existence. Given this, it is surprising that we don't devote more time to learning how to make contact with others. With an understanding of ourselves and the ways we communicate, along with a knowledge of the basics of successful communication, we can have more rewarding interpersonal interactions whenever we are meeting someone new, are engaged in conversation, are interviewing for a job, or are expressing our needs and desires to others.

Chapter Three

Listening Skills

Listen Up

There is an old adage that we have two ears and one mouth so we can listen twice as much as we talk. In actuality, this is almost the case. Research by the Sperry Corporation reveals that, of the time we spend communicating throughout the course of our lives, we devote more time to listening than speaking, reading, or writing. In fact, roughly half of our communicative time is spent on listening (Adler, 89). We listen to the television and the radio, while in classes, at public lectures and speeches, at concerts, during interviews, and in conversation. Still, even though so much time is spent on listening, significantly less classroom time is spent teaching this skill than the other skills of communication.

When Lyndon Johnson was in the Senate, he had a sign on the wall of his office which plainly expressed the importance of listening. It read, "When you're talking, you ain't learning" (Qubein, 95). David P. Reynolds, chairman of Reynolds Aluminum, points out, "The ability to communicate and listen effectively is probably the most important skill at a manager's command because all other management skills depend on it" (Franklin and Clark, 39).

Anecdotal evidence also demonstrates the significance of effective listening. Nido R. Qubein tells the story of a young man who, many years ago, went to Western Union seeking a job (95-96). In that day, messages were transmitted in Morse code via the telegraph. Though the young man had studied telegraphy at home and had learned the code, he had no experience and realized his chances of getting the job were slim when he walked in the office and saw a crowd of people filling out applications. Still, he decided to fill out an application. As he was doing so, he heard a clicking noise in the background. He immediately stopped filling out his form and listened. Then he ran into a nearby office. Moments later, an official of Western Union emerged from that office and told the other applicants that the job had been filled and they could go home. You see, the clicking noise was the sound of a telegraph sending out the message, "If you understand this, come into the office. The job is yours." Because the young man had the ability to listen and to understand, he got the job.

Listening skills are still vital for professionals today. In the book *Essentials of Speech Communication*, Sharon Franklin and Deborah J. Clark tell of Kay Hunter, who is a successful garden designer (39). The reason for her success? She knows how to listen. When she first meets with clients, Hunter spends an hour listening to what they want their gardens to look like and the problems they should solve. She shows her clients pictures of various plants and pays careful attention to their responses. Further, she always asks numerous questions so she is sure of her client's likes and dislikes. Hunter's occupation isn't exceptional. Many career fields demand outstanding listening skills. Doctors can't heal their patients if they don't listen to the symptoms they describe; architects, photographers, and interior designers must listen to ascertain the needs and desires of their clients; attorneys must listen carefully to their clients as they describe their problems and their opponents in a trial so they may argue effectively against them; counselors and psychologists spend most of their day listening to patients. In short, listening skills are vital to both personal and professional success.

What Listening Is Not — Common Misconceptions

Perhaps the best way to understand what listening *is* is to understand what it *is not*. The following are common misconceptions about listening:

- **Hearing is the same as listening.** Hearing, the physical reception of sound waves by auditory mechanisms, is the first step in the listening process. But it is possible to hear and not to listen. To listen, you must also understand by paying attention to those sounds and organizing them into a meaningful pattern. We hear all the time without listening. For instance, we often block out background noise, such as traffic, when we are involved in something else such as a conversation or a television show. Or, has someone ever had to call to you a number of times to get your attention because you were reading or deep in thought? It's not because you couldn't hear them, it's because you weren't listening to them.

- **Listening happens naturally — all you have to do is sit back and let the sound waves enter your ears.** Not true. In actuality, listening is an active, not a passive, process. Good listeners understand that listening actually takes a great deal of effort and energy. In the book *How to Speak, How to Listen*, Mortimer J. Adler draws an analogy between a listener and a catcher in a baseball game (86). Though the catcher receives the pitch, he must be actively involved in the play or the ball will hit him in the head. Likewise, in order to adequately receive a message, a listener must be actively involved.

- **How much you remember determines how well you remember.** Nope. Simply being able to record and regurgitate information does not mean that you listened. Effective listeners also analyze the message they hear, searching for meaning.

- **Listening is a skill that is acquired naturally and cannot be taught.** Wrong again. Just because we listen often doesn't mean we listen well. Knowing the factors that prevent us from listening well and methods for effective listening can help us become better listeners.

Types of Listening

We don't always listen with the same objective. Rather, listening skills depend on the purpose of our listening.

Informational Listening

We often listen to gain and evaluate information. We listen for information in classes, in business meetings, when we watch an educational program on television (like a news report), when we are being trained for a new job, and when we are receiving advice.

Critical Listening

A second purpose of listening is to make judgments of people and ideas. While we must gain information while listening critically, this type of listening goes beyond simply gathering facts. Critical listening requires that we analyze and evaluate that information as well as the individuals to whom we are listening. For instance, when we are watching two candidates for public office debate, we are evaluating the merit of their arguments and ideas as well as the quality of their character and leadership abilities.

Empathic Listening

Also called relationship listening, the purpose of this type of listening is to demonstrate care and concern for a friend by listening to them describe their problems or worries.

Appreciative Listening

Sometimes we listen just for pleasure, like when we listen to music, watch a comedian, or when an acquaintance tells us a joke or an interesting story. Though this type of listening does not require as much skill as the other types of listening, you may not get as much out of the message if you don't practice the techniques of effective listening.

Discriminative Listening

A final reason we listen is to discriminate between fine differences in sounds. When a car mechanic listens to an engine to identify the cause of a malfunction, or when a mother listens to her baby's cry to determine the reason for his or her unhappiness, they are practicing discriminative listening.

Barriers to Effective Listening

The first step in becoming an effective listener is to understand the factors that get in our way when we attempt to listen. These factors are called barriers, or obstacles. Barriers to effective listening are categorized as internal, external, cultural, or from the speaker. Internal barriers are factors that exist within the listener, such as an unwillingness to listen or a tendency to daydream; external barriers are environmental interference from outside the listener such as noise, other distracting stimuli, or information overload; cultural barriers arise from differences in culture between the speaker and the listener and include prejudice, vocabulary, and accents; and speaker barriers are problems caused by the speaker, like a sloppy appearance, a lack of credibility, or a less than captivating message.

Forms of Ineffective Listening

While barriers and distractions make listening difficult, we often worsen the situation by listening ineffectively or practicing tactics that allow us to appear to be listening when, in actuality, we are not. The following are common tendencies that all of us, at one time or another, commit, preventing us from effective listening:

Lack of Effort

Often, we aren't willing to invest the time and effort it takes to listen to another person. Students often come to class more intent on writing a note to a friend, daydreaming, or getting a jump-start on a homework assignment for another class than ·on focusing carefully on the teacher's lecture. Parents are often unwilling to put the newspaper down to attend to something their child may be trying to say. Sometimes we may intend to listen carefully, but become bored by a speaker, which quells our enthusiasm for listening.

Pseudolistening

Pseudolistening is pretending to listen. When we practice this tactic, we appear to be listening, but our minds are really far away. We pseudolisten in situations when communication bores us but we are obliged to appear interested, such as a boring lecture by a teacher or a boss or a superficial conversation. Obviously, this can be dangerous. If you are practicing pseuodolistening during a lecture, for instance, you run the risk of being called on by the teacher and not being able to provide an answer.

Monopolizing

When someone hogs the conversation, constantly interrupts, and continually focuses discussion on himself, he is monopolizing the conversation and is inevitably not listening.

Preoccupation

Another hindrance to listening occurs when we are so absorbed with a thought or a concern that we can't focus on what someone is saying. Once, when I was in high school, I had a big basketball game right after school. As the day progressed and I grew more and more excited about the game, I paid less and less attention to my teachers.

Prejudgments

When we believe that we know what someone will say, or believe that a speaker is not worth listening to, we are making prejudgments that prevent us from listening well. For instance, if you work with someone who always makes useless suggestions, you may tune out every time he speaks in a meeting. Doing so, however, may cause you to miss the one good idea he presents. Or perhaps you may see a speaker and decide, before he says a word, that he looks like a geek. You may not listen carefully to his speech because of your prejudgment and may miss out on someone whose ideas could be of great benefit to you.

Rehearsing

When you plan what you will say next instead of listening to the person who currently has the floor, the quality of your listening suffers.

Mind Reading

Rather than taking what people say at face value, the mind reader tries to figure out what the speaker is really thinking and feeling. "She says she wants to go out, but she looks stressed. I'll bet she really wants to stay home."

Selective Listening

When you listen selectively, or filter, you either listen for specific information and then stop paying attention after you hear what you were waiting for, or you only hear what you want to hear. A father might want to know how his daughter performed at a soccer game, but will only pretend to pay attention when she describes the performance of her teammates. Or, if a teacher begins critiquing a student by saying, "You really researched your paper well, but ..." the student may focus on the compliment and ignore the criticism that follows.

Identifying

Have you ever talked to someone who, for every experience you related, had a similar experience to tell you about? You tell about your trip to the beach, they tell you how they used to live in a condo that overlooked the beach. You tell them about a picture you painted, they tell you about their masterpiece. That person is an identifier. These individuals do not listen well because they relate everything in a conversation to their own experience.

Advising

"Advisors" see themselves as problem solvers. After hearing a few sentences, they stop focusing on the speaker's message and begin to think of suggestions and solutions to help the speaker. However, because they don't listen carefully, advisors can't empathize with the speaker, may not fully understand a problem, and offer advice when it is not wanted.

Sparring

Some of us enjoy friendly debate. However, when you try to argue with every point another person makes, either directly or through more subtle means, you are not really listening to that person or trying to understand them.

Opinionatedness

Sometimes we refuse to listen because we believe we are right. Thus, we don't hear criticism or correction.

Derailing

Another barrier to listening is derailing a conversation by suddenly changing the topic when you become bored or uncomfortable. Humor is one way to derail a conversation. Many people, when confronted with a situation that makes them uncomfortable, use a joke to either lighten the mood or to cover their true feelings.

Placating

When you placate, you agree with everything the speaker says so you don't have to pay careful attention. Also called humoring, you go along with the speaker, oftentimes short-circuiting the conversation.

Active Listening

As we have already noted, listening is not a passive process. Effective listeners are active participants in the communication process. The following steps are involved in active listening:

- **Be mindful.** The first step in effective listening is carefully paying attention. Devote your full attention to the speaker, stay focused on the message, and avoid daydreaming.

- **Eliminate barriers.** As much as possible, eliminate both internal barriers (by having the proper attitude toward listening) and external barriers (by choosing a quiet spot, blocking out distractions, and creating a comfortable environment for communication).

- **Paraphrase.** The next step in the process of active listening is to restate what someone has said in your own words. This technique forces you to try to understand what the other person means, helps you remember what they say, prevents you from practicing ineffective listening tendencies, and lets speakers know they have been heard. Phrases such as, "In other words," "You seem to be saying," "Let me see if I've got this right," and "Do you mean?" can be used as lead-ins to paraphrases.

- **Clarify.** Clarifying is simply asking questions until you gain a fuller understanding of what the speaker is saying. Not only does this technique help you fill in missing information, it also lets the speaker know that you're interested in what they have to say.

- **Provide Feedback.** In Chapter One of this text, the communication process is discussed. An important part of that process is feedback, the reactions of listeners to the source of communication. Providing feedback is also a vital part of active listening. When given in a nonjudgmental way, feedback helps other people understand the effect of their messages, allows you to correct errors and misconceptions, and provides you with an opportunity to express your point of view. According to McKay, Davis, and Fanning, there are three important rules for providing feedback: it must be immediate, honest, and supportive (25). It is possible to express your feelings in a gentle, tactful way that doesn't cause defensiveness.

- **Listen with your entire body.** Nonverbals can provide support and feedback. While you listen, make direct eye contact and lean toward the speaker, nod your head to demonstrate understanding, and smile. Avoid body language that reveals boredom or a desire to be somewhere else, like glancing at your watch, fidgeting, and looking toward the door.

When practicing informational or critical listening, remember:

- **Take notes.** Not only does this provide a reference for you to consult later, the very act of taking notes helps you pay attention and retain information.

- **Organize information.** We remember information that is structured more easily than information given in random order. Therefore, when you are listening to a presentation, a demonstration, a lecture, or to evaluate a message, it will help you if you regroup and restructure what you hear. Try to identify the main idea and the major supporting points and then group information under those points.

- **Ask yourself key questions.** While you listen, ask the following questions: Are any internal or external barriers preventing me from listening effectively? What do I know about the speaker? How believable do I find the speaker? Does the speaker seem prepared? Are the ideas presented logical? Is the presentation well organized? Is the evidence offered sufficient? Is the evidence from credible sources? These queries will help you evaluate messages more critically.

Identifying Breakdowns in Logic

Effective listening involves more than simply knowing how to listen. To evaluate the quality of a message, you must analyze that message to discern its quality and merit. A knowledge of common logical fallacies, or errors in reasoning, and propaganda techniques, can help you to do so.

Common Logical Fallacies

- **Name calling.** When a speaker slaps an unfavorable label on another person or idea without providing evidence or reasoning to justify the use of that term, they are committing this fallacy. Politicians do this all the time, applying terms like "right-wing extremist" or "environmental wacko" to create preconceptions and prejudice toward their opponents.

- **Card stacking.** Instead of presenting all relevant information, the speaker only provides the facts that support the point he or she is trying to make. Just as a magician carefully arranges a deck of cards to make a trick work, a speaker committing this fallacy hides some information while placing more favorable facts at the top of the deck.

- **Hasty generalization.** When speakers draw a conclusion from just a few examples, they commit this fallacy. For instance, if you watch an NFL game in which the quarterback completes only one pass in ten attempts and also throws an interception, you might conclude that player does not have a future in the league. However, one game is not enough to judge the quality of a player. If you were a coach who discounted the player in this example, for instance, you might have cut John Elway as those were his statistics in his first professional game.

- **Glittering generality.** This fallacy occurs when the source uses a word or phrase that carries favorable connotation but is actually so vague no one can really agree on what it means. By doing so, they create a positive impression of their ideas, even if they have nothing to do with the concept you think they support. For example, Nike's slogan "Just Do It" sounds like a good idea because we value action. When you stop to think about it, though, you wonder: Just do what? Exercise? Buy a $150 pair of shoes? Wear your underwear outside your pants? We don't know what they really mean.

- **Begging the question.** When your support and premises depend on each other to be proven, or you use a self-defining proposition, you are begging the question. Tim Dowling writes in *Men's Health* magazine that you can learn a lot about begging the question from driving instructors. For instance, a driving instructor may say that good drivers keep their hands in the "ten and two" position. However, as Dowling says:

  > "You may try to refute him by saying you know some very good drivers who put their hands at something more like 20 past 7. Virtually every driving instructor will smugly reply that anyone who does that is not a good driver. Since he has used his proposition as the definition for one of its terms, i.e. that a good driver is defined as someone who grips the wheel at 10 and 2, you may rightly shout at him, 'That begs the question about six ways from Sunday, you bald jerk!'" (61)

- **False premises.** If you start with a claim that is not true or not proven, you cannot draw any credible conclusions from it. For instance, if you argue that, "Since Millard Fillmore was the best president our country has ever had, his policies are beyond criticism," you are working on a false premise since you never proved Fillmore to be the best president in American history.

- **Post hoc.** Erroneous cause-effect arguments contain the post hoc fallacy, which occurs when someone assumes that when one event precedes another in time, it causes the other. For instance, I may observe that, since birds fly south before winter comes each year, the birds flying south actually cause the beginning of winter.

47

- **Non sequitur.** A Latin term meaning "it does not follow," a non sequitur occurs when a conclusion is drawn from facts that don't really support it. An advertisement in which a spokesperson claims, "I'm in great shape. If you want to feel as good as I do, buy the Gruntalot Weight Machine," contains a non sequitur because the fact that the spokesperson is in great shape may have nothing to do with the weight machine.

- **Tu Quoque argument.** Literally translated as "you are another," this fallacy occurs when someone deflects blame by pointing out fault with others. For instance, if a politician is accused of wrongdoing, he may argue that other politicians have been doing the same thing for years. Still, the guilt of others doesn't make this politician any less guilty himself.

- **Stereotypes.** Often, a persuasive appeal will play on preconceived notions about a person based on his or her membership in a group. However, any right thinking individual knows that people are individuals and cannot be so easily categorized.

Common Propaganda Techniques

Used often by advertisers, propaganda involves manipulative persuasive techniques that elicit an emotional response and do not allow listeners to make a rational, considered decision.

- **Transfer.** Making an illogical comparison between unrelated things is transfer. Advertisers use this technique to create favorable impressions of their product. For instance, a commercial for bath soap may show a woman frolicking in a field full of wildflowers, trying to transfer that feeling to their soap.

- **Testimonial.** Testimonials use a well-known individual as a spokesperson for a certain product. Tiger Woods, for instance, endorses Buick automobiles, even though he is not a mechanic nor has any expert knowledge of cars.

- **Bandwagon.** The premise that since everyone is doing

something you should too is the bandwagon technique. Assuming the listener will follow the crowd, this propaganda technique plays on our desire to belong.

Are You a Good Listener? Take this Quiz and Find Out!

To test your listening skills, take this quiz adapted from *How to Be a Great Communicator*, by Nido R. Qubein (105-06). Answer each question as honestly as possible. For each question, score yourself on the following scale:

1=never 2=rarely 3=sometimes 4=most of the time 5=always

1. I try to give each person I converse with as much time to talk as I take.
2. I truly enjoy hearing what other people have to say.
3. Rather than being anxious to speak myself, I can wait until someone else finishes what they have to say.
4. I avoid interrupting others.
5. I listen carefully to the message, even if I don't like the person who is speaking.
6. I don't judge other's ideas by their sex or age.
7. I assume every person has something worthwhile to say and am equally interested in listening to friends, acquaintances, and strangers.
8. I put away whatever I am doing and focus my attention completely on the speaker to whom I am listening.
9. I put preoccupations aside to give the speaker my full attention.
10. In conversation, I ask questions to gain more information.
11. I provide feedback to speakers.
12. I respond to speakers nonverbally.
13. I ask for clarification if a speaker says something I don't understand.
14. I ask myself critical questions when I listen to speeches and presentations.

15. I structure a message mentally, identifying the central idea and the main points.

16. I take notes when listening to a lecture, speech, or presentation.

17. I respect each person's right to their opinion, even if I disagree with them.

18. I look for points on which I can agree with the speaker, even if I disagree with their overall premise.

19. I view disagreements and disputes as an opportunity to understand the other person better.

20. I recognize that listening is a skill I can develop with knowledge and practice.

Scoring

90–100: Wow! You deserve one of life's greatest compliments: "You're a great listener."

80–89: You're a good listener, but there's room for improvement.

70–79: Your listening needs work — you're missing out on a lot of important information.

below 70: Ouch! Your listening skills need some serious work.

Conclusion

William Shakespeare advised us to "Give every man thy ear but few thy voice." Communication cannot occur without listening. When we understand the barriers and blocks that hinder listening as well as the techniques of active listening and how to recognize fallacious arguments and propaganda techniques, we can significantly improve our communication skills.

Chapter Four

Nonverbal Communication

When you engage in conversation with others, what do you think is more important: their words or their actions? While most people would say that an individual's words have the most impact, research shows otherwise. A landmark 1968 study by Albert Mehrabian (McKay, Davis, and Fanning, 59) breaks down the total impact of a message as follows:

7%	verbal (the words spoken)
38%	vocalics (volume, pitch, rhythm, etc.)
55%	body movements (facial expressions, gestures, posture)

Don't believe it? Consider this situation: You ask your friend how her day is going. She says, "Fine," but sighs and slumps her shoulders as she says it. You'll probably ignore her answer and ask her what's wrong. Or consider a teacher who chides a student for telling a joke in class, but struggles to conceal a grin. The class will conclude that, even though the teacher felt obligated to reprimand the student for disrupting the class, he really found the joke funny. As journalist Bill Briggs says, "It's not what you say or how you say it — it's what your body is doing while your tongue is wagging" (E1).

Not only is the study of nonverbal communication important and indispensable, it is also fascinating. Countless articles are written each year on issues such as body language, personal space, the meaning of different types of touch, the importance of physical attractiveness, and time management. Hopefully, you will find the information in this chapter interesting as you gain a better understanding of yourself and others.

What Is Nonverbal Communication?

When you hear the phrase "nonverbal communication," you probably think of gestures and body language. In fact, "body language" and "nonverbals" are often used interchangeably. In actuality, the field of nonverbal communication is much more broad. How we say words (through the use of inflection and volume), the way we dress, our environments, the way we use touch, and the way we use time are all examples of nonverbal behaviors. In their book, *Nonverbal Behavior in Interpersonal Relations*, Virginia P. Richmond and James C. McCroskey define nonverbal communication as "the process of one person stimulating meaning in the mind of another person or persons by means of nonverbal messages" (1). All aspects of communication other than words can be classified as nonverbal.

Though this seems obvious, there are many myths and misconceptions about nonverbal communication. Richmond and McCroskey identify the following (2-3):

Myths about Nonverbal Communication

- **There is no such thing as nonverbal communication.** Many people believe that communication involves language and, therefore, nonverbal communication is not a legitimate field of study. In fact, it is impossible to separate verbal and nonverbal communication. When you speak, your gestures and facial expressions accentuate your words. Even when speaking on the phone, your tone of voice, rate, volume, and inflection affects the meaning.

- **If you understand nonverbal communication, you can almost read others like a book.** It's almost as if people believe they can read someone's mind if they know the secret of interpreting nonverbal behaviors. We've all seen the headlines. "Is She Interested? Her Body Language Will Tell You!" In one episode of a popular television show, one character read a book on interpreting body language. He proceeded to tell everyone he encountered exactly what they were thinking by simply looking at them. Of course, he was invariably wrong. The reason this doesn't work is that human behavior is not structured like a language. It can only be interpreted in a context. If someone shakes his fist, for instance, he may be celebrating, expressing anger, or threatening someone else. Because of this, another misconception about nonverbal communication is that ...

- **Nonverbal behaviors always mean the same thing.** Since nonverbal behaviors must be interpreted within a context, this is simply not true. As the ancient philosopher Plutarch says, "It is circumstance and proper measure that give an action its character."

- **You can tell if a person is lying by looking at them.** This goes along with the last two misconceptions. If you can't tell what someone is thinking just by looking at them, how can you tell if they are telling the truth? Some people say that, if someone doesn't look you in the eye while they speak to you, they must be lying. This doesn't make sense. Someone may avoid eye contact out of shyness, or you may purposely make direct eye contact to make a lie more convincing. Simply, nonverbal communication is not a secret code!

- **Nonverbal behaviors are natural and cannot be learned.** If this were true, nonverbal behaviors would remain constant across cultures. They don't. In fact, books have been written helping travelers learn differences in body language and proper nonverbal etiquette in other countries and cultures. In 1991, when President George Bush visited Australia, he showed what he thought was the international symbol of peace (two fingers forming a V) through the window of his limo, but his hand was turned the wrong way. In Australia, this means roughly the same thing as an upraised middle finger in America! This famous gaffe demonstrates that many gestures and expressions are taught and ingrained within us by our culture.

Functions of Nonverbal Communication

So, now that we know what nonverbal communication is *not*, let's try to figure out what it *is*. Perhaps the best way to do this is to examine why we use nonverbals. Following are the six different functions of nonverbal communication:

- **Substituting.** We sometimes use nonverbals instead of talking. This occurs any time an action replaces a word. Examples of substituting can range from simple gestures, like a wave or a thumbs-up, to more complex motions, such as sign language.

- **Reinforcing.** This occurs when we use nonverbals to complement a verbal message. If you nod your head while saying, "Yes," or pound the table while you berate someone, you are reinforcing verbal messages with gestures. When your nonverbals have roughly the same meaning as what you say, you are said to have congruence, which many believe essential for skillful nonverbal communication.

- **Contradicting.** Sometimes, instead of reinforcing the verbal message, we use nonverbals to contradict, dispute, or counter what we are saying. If a child tells her parents that she is sorry, but does so with a pout and a sneer, her facial expressions will betray her words. Sarcasm is perhaps the most common example of how we contradict verbal messages with nonverbals. By using sarcasm, we intentionally give our true meaning away through our tone of voice and body movements.

- **Regulating.** We also use nonverbals to regulate, or coordinate, verbal interactions. Consider, for instance, a high school or college class. The instructor may signal the class to be quiet through a pointed look while students raise their hands if they wish to speak and provide nonverbal feedback to show the teacher that they are bored, confused, or ready to move on. Finally, the teacher will realize that class is about to end as students begin to close their books and put their materials in their backpacks.

- **Managing Impressions.** The fifth reason we use nonverbals is to control the way others perceive us. In large part, we make decisions about our hair style, our clothes, the car we drive, the way we walk, and even the tone of voice we use in order to influence how we are seen by others. Think about how carefully you choose what you will wear to a job interview or a date. You do this because you are using nonverbals (your clothes) to make a good impression.

- **Establishing Relationships.** Finally, nonverbals help us establish and define relationships. We hold hands to show that we are in love and wear wedding bands to show we are married. In a business meeting, the CEO may sit at the head of the table to show he is in charge.

It is important to realize that these functions do not always occur independently. Instead, one nonverbal message can accomplish many purposes simultaneously. Also, verbal messages usually serve a content function while nonverbals primarily serve a relational or affective purpose. This means that we say what we think, but we show how we feel.

Types of Nonverbal Communication

As mentioned earlier, the field of nonverbal communication is broad and varied. Far more than gestures and body movements, there are numerous types of nonverbal messages. We will consider the following:

- Kinesics (gestures and body movement)
- Facial Behavior
- Proxemics (personal space and territory)
- Haptics (touch)
- Paralanguage
- Environment and Physical Surroundings
- Chronemics (perception and use of time)
- Artifacts (personal objects)
- Appearance

Kinesics

Big words do not smite like war-clubs,
Boastful breath is not a bow string,
Taunts are not so sharp as arrows,

Deeds are better things than words are,
Actions mightier than boastings.
> — Henry Wadsworth Longfellow,
> *The Song of Hiawatha, Part ix.*

It has often been said that actions speak louder than words. If this is true, the study of kinesics, a technical term for gestures and body movement, is vital. Virginia P. Richmond and James C. McCroskey assert that "Gestures and body movements often convey a person's true feeling behind her or his words" (52). Gestures, posture, and movement of any part of the body can all be classified as kinesic behavior.

There are five types of body movements: emblems, illustrators, affect displays, regulators, and adaptors.

Emblems

While most gestures have no specific meaning, some do. In America, most people understand the specific gestures for "OK," "peace," and "hello." These gestures that directly translate into words or phrases and can actually serve as nonverbal substitutes for words are called emblems. In order to be considered an emblem, a gesture or movement must have a direct verbal translation, be known by most people in a group or culture, and be used intentionally by individuals to send a specific message to an individual or group.

Perhaps the most commonly used and best known emblem is the display of the middle finger, also known as "the bird." This gesture is so widely used and known that authors M.J. Loheed, Matt Patterson, and Eddie Schmidt wrote an entire book on this one gesture. (If you're interested, and I hope you're not, it's called *The Finger: A Comprehensive Guide to Flipping Off*). If the authors are to be believed, this gesture can be traced back to the ancient Greeks and has been used by such luminaries as the Roman Emperor Caligula, Supreme Court Justice William Brennan, and Vice President Nelson Rockefeller. Many athletes, such as baseball player Albert Belle and football star Brian Cox, have made national headlines by showing their middle fingers to fans. This would not have happened had not everyone known the exact meaning of this gesture.

Because emblems operate as words, they are as arbitrary as any word in any language and do not always remain the same across cultures. Though officially classified as nonverbal communication, emblems have more in common with verbal communication than any other type of nonverbal behavior.

Illustrators

Often called "speech-linked gestures," illustrators are nonverbal behaviors that accompany and literally "illustrate" verbal messages. Usually intentional, they are more natural than emblems but cannot stand alone or replace the verbal message. For instance, if you ask someone to wait, you might illustrate the idea by extending your hand with the palm turned toward them. As you might expect, research has found that illustrators are used more in face-to-face interaction. Still, we become so used to using illustrators that we often gesture when speaking to someone we can't see (like when we are on the phone). Research has also found that communication is smoother, more fluent, and less confusing when illustrators are used "in sync" with speech.

Affect Displays

Primarily facial expressions, but also including posture, the way a person walks, and other movements, affect displays are nonverbal behaviors that reveal emotional meaning. Affect displays are often unintentional (like a look of surprise) but can also be intended or created. In fact, we're usually very good at faking an emotion when we want to. Have you ever laughed at a joke that wasn't funny to be polite? Pretended to be surprised when playing "peekaboo" with a child? If so, you have created affect displays.

Regulators

Regulators are gestures and movements that control, maintain, and regulate interactions. We use these nonverbals to tell others what to expect or what we want them to do while we're speaking. Primary among regulators are turn-taking behaviors, which are nonverbal behaviors that help control the flow of conversation. They are broken down into the following categories:

- **Turn-yielding cues** are gestures and movements that indicate you have finished speaking and are ready to listen. Examples of yielding cues are a beckoning gesture, a forward lean, silence, and vocal inflection (such as a questioning intonation that indicates a response is desired).

- **Turn-maintaining cues** are the opposite of yielding cues. They are used by speakers who wish to signal to others that they want to continue speaking. For instance, you may fill a pause with an "um," to indicate that you have not yet finished your thought or hold up your hand to prevent someone else from taking the floor.

- **Turn-requesting regulators** differ from yielding and maintaining cues in that they are used by listeners to signal the speaker that they would like to speak. The most obvious example of a turn-requesting regulator is a student raising his or her hand, but shifting posture, an audible intake of breath, or clearing the throat can also accomplish the same purpose.

- **Turn-denying regulators**, such as silence, positive head nods, and short utterances like "uh-huh" and "I see," are used to tell others that we don't want a turn and that they should continue speaking.

Adaptors

Adaptors are coping behaviors that satisfy some physical or emotional need, such as scratching an itch, fidgeting with a pen or pencil, or wringing hands together. Adaptors are broken down into three categories:

- **Self-adaptors** are, as the name suggests, done to your own body. Scratching, rubbing, and hair-twisting are all self-adaptors.

- **Alter-directed adaptors** are movements that, often subconsciously, protect us from others. For example, we may fold our arms to close ourselves to someone or to protect us from a verbal attack.

- **Object-focused adaptors** are the unconscious manipulations of objects, such as biting a pen, smoking, or fidgeting with jewelry.

What Does Your Posture Communicate?

When I was young, my mother was continually nagging me to "stand up straight" and to "hold my head up." Though I became annoyed with her admonishments, they were founded in sound theory. My mother realized that the way we walk, sit, and stand reveals much about our mood as well as our general self-esteem. Slumped posture is associated with feelings of fatigue, depression, and a sense of inferiority, while a tall posture is considered a sign of happiness, confidence, openness to others, and high self-esteem.

Albert Scheflen, a noted writer and researcher in the area of kinesics, identifies three ways we communicate through posture (Richmond and McCroskey, 67). First, we use posture to show if we are inclusive or noninclusive. A group of three people engaged in conversation may form a tight circle, indicating they are not open to others. Secondly, according to Scheflen, we reveal ourselves by either placing ourselves parallel or face to face with the person to whom we are talking. Two people engaged in conversation while standing or sitting side-by-side are usually equals who are involved in a passive conversation, while those who converse facing each other are typically engaged in a more formal, professional discussion or are more actively immersed in the discourse.

Finally, Scheflen argues that we can tell much about individuals involved in an interaction by examining whether their posture is congruent (similar to each other) or incongruent (markedly different). Congruent posture shared by two individuals can indicate equality, agreement, and liking. However, incongruent posture usually indicates that one person is of higher status than the other. In a job interview, who is more likely to lean back or slouch in a chair? Who would you expect to see seated on the edge of the chair, leaning forward? Most likely, the interviewer, who has higher status, would be more relaxed while the applicant would be more tense and respectful.

What Is Your Communicator Style?

Robert Norton, in his 1983 book *Communicator Style: Theory, Applications, and Measures*, asserts that each person has a communicator style, which is defined as the predominant manner or style in which a person communicates. The communicator style gives form to the content of a message and signals how the literal meaning should be taken, interpreted, or understood.

Norton identifies nine primary communicator styles: dramatic, dominant, animated, relaxed, attentive, open, friendly, contentious, and impression-leaving. The style we use when communicating affects the way we are perceived by others. For instance, people who use the dramatic style are seen as more popular, attractive, and important, while those who are relaxed communicators are believed to demonstrate self-confidence and assurance. Richmond and McCroskey cite studies that show teachers' communicator styles affects the way they are seen by students (72). Teachers who were rated as dramatic are seen as more effective by their students (probably because they are more interesting speakers), while attentive and open teachers are perceived as more caring and supportive.

Facial Behavior

The next time you watch a movie or television, look specifically for shots that show only an actor's face. You'll be surprised how many close-ups are used. You'll also be surprised at how adept many actors are at conveying emotion and meaning using only facial expressions. This is possible because the face is the most expressive part of the body. In fact, communications expert Mario Pei estimates that the face is capable of 250,000 different expressions (McCutcheon, Schaffer, and Wycoff, 79). Clichés such as, "I can read it in your face," and "the eyes are the window of the soul," demonstrate our belief in the expressiveness of the face.

Given this, you would think that our facial expressions would be a dead give-away as to our emotions. Not true. We realize that our face can show emotion and therefore become experts at masking our feelings. In fact, we learn to control our facial behavior very early in life. To accomplish this, we use the following facial management techniques:

Facial Management Techniques
• **Masking** occurs when we replace the emotion we are really

feeling with the expression of the emotion we are supposed to be feeling. For instance, when you lose a contest, you might feel disappointment or anger. Instead, you smile and congratulate the winner because that is the socially acceptable response.

- **Intensification** of our expressions occurs when we exaggerate what we really feel. Again, we usually do so to fulfill social expectations and norms. If someone tells a joke that you find mildly amusing, you might laugh heartily out of courtesy. If you do, you are intensifying the emotion of slight amusement you feel.

- **Neutralization** can be likened to a poker face. When we neutralize, we don't exhibit the emotion we feel. Though it may sometimes be difficult, there are many times it is to our benefit to hide emotion.

- **Deintensification** is, as you might expect, the opposite of intensification. This technique involves deemphasizing the emotion we really feel to meet societal norms. You may hold back tears because you don't want to cry in public or restrain your anger so that you may express it in a more productive way.

Facial Feedback Hypothesis

Obviously, the reason we use facial management techniques is to fool others. Oddly, we may also be fooling ourselves when we control our facial expressions. Researchers have developed the facial feedback hypothesis, which states that our facial expressions affect the degree to which we become emotionally aroused. Studies show that people who exaggerate facial expressions demonstrate higher physiological arousal than those who suppress them, while people who don't exaggerate or suppress their emotions fall somewhere in the middle in terms of emotional arousal. For instance, in one study, subjects were asked to view sad photographs while simulating a sad expression. The results showed that this actually increased the sadness the subjects felt as they looked at the photographs. So it is possible to affect ourselves while we attempt to influence the way others perceive us.

Eye Behavior

Their eyes met across a crowded room. She knew in an instant that he was the man for her ...

No, the above sentence is not the beginning of a romance novel, but it could be an actual occurrence. Far more than enabling us to see, the human eye is a potent communicative tool. With our eyes, we can show amusement, anger, love, hate, disgust, and interest. In fact, you've probably had the experience of communicating with someone simply by looking at them. For this reason, it behooves us to study how we communicate with our eyes.

Our eyes serve many communicative functions. They allow us to scan and gain information about the world around us, to establish and define relationships (usually accomplished through eye contact), to obligate others to interact with us, to control and regulate our interactions with others, and to express emotions. In fact, unlike other facial expressions, it is very difficult for us to control our eye behavior, making the eyes one of the most reliable sources of information about an individual's emotional state.

Even the pupils of the eye communicate as they dilate (become larger) and constrict (become smaller). Researchers have found that pupil dilation can be a sign of emotional arousal and interest. In one study, subject's pupils dilated when they were shown pictures of attractive members of the opposite sex. Further, pupil dilation can affect perceptions of attractiveness. In one study, subjects were shown two identical pictures of the same woman, one with her pupils dilated and one with them constricted. The subjects found the model more attractive when her eyes were dilated (Richmond and McCroskey, 98-99). Italian women of the fourteenth and fifteenth century realized this. They put drops of belladonna into their eyes to dilate the pupils so that they would look more attractive. Of course, factors such as the brightness of the room can affect pupil size, and it is often impossible to see the pupils of another person's eyes, so it is difficult to read too much into observations of pupil dilation.

Eye contact can reveal a great deal about the nature of a relationship. A lower status individual (such as an employee) will look more at a higher status person (such as the boss). This may be done as a sign of respect or of a perceived need to monitor the feedback of the higher status individual. Eye contact also seems to increase more when people like each other. For example, the amount of eye contact between spouses corresponds with the degree to which they are happy in their marriage. Finally, studies have found that women look at their conversation partners more often than men. Theorists believe this is to satisfy their higher need for inclusion, affiliation, and affection. Finally, eye contact is treated differently in different cultures. While it is considered a sign of respect for children to make eye contact with adults in America, other cultures teach children not to look at adults or at individuals of a higher status.

Proxemics

I once had a friend who always stood too close to people when speaking to them. As he crowded others, you could see them back away and look uncomfortable. The problem was that my friend did not understand the culturally acceptable way to use proxemics, which is the study of space and how we use it to communicate.

Anthropologists believe that we all have an invisible bubble of "personal space" that surrounds us and that we become uncomfortable if someone invades that private territory. This bubble expands and contracts depending on the situation and who we are with. We have a much smaller bubble of personal space when with a loved one than when we are talking to an acquaintance, for instance. Because of this, much can be learned about relationships by examining the way interactants use personal space.

Types of Space

- **The intimate zone.** From touching to eighteen inches, this distance is used for confidential exchanges and is reserved for close friends, family members, and lovers. A boyfriend and girlfriend talk while holding each other close; children sit on the lap of a parent when reading.

- **The personal zone.** From eighteen inches to about four feet, this space is used for conversations between close friends and relatives.

- **The social zone.** The ordinary distance people maintain for most social and business interactions, the social zone ranges from four to twelve feet.

- **The public zone.** We try to stay twelve feet or more from people we encounter in public places like a shopping mall or on the street.

While the numbers given above represent averages, the personal space used by individuals varies according to gender and culture. Studies reveal that females tend to interact with others at a closer distance than do males, but a man and a woman will typically stand closer to each other than will two women or two men. If you've ever been to another country, you've probably realized that culture also affects the amount of personal space individuals use. I learned this when I went to see a movie in Europe. Though the theatre was mostly empty, as was the row in which I was sitting, a man who entered sat in the chair right next to me. In America, people almost invariably leave an empty space between them and the person next to them when it is possible to do so. In general, America is considered a "non-contact culture" because we tend to protect a larger area of personal space than people in many other parts of the world.

Territory

If you've ever watched the Discovery Channel, you know that animals often claim and mark territory. Humans are no different. We also stake claims to areas, sometimes when we have no formal or legal reason to do so. Your territory could be your home, your office, your locker at school, or even a section of sand where you place your towel at the beach.

Territories can be classified into different types:

- **Body territory** is personal space, which has already been discussed.

- **Primary territory** is area that belongs exclusively to its owner. Offices, bedrooms, work areas, and dorm rooms are considered primary territory.

- **Secondary territory** does not belong to the person or group who claims it, but is generally associated with them. For instance, if a group of high school friends always meets in the same spot in the hall between classes, that area is considered their secondary territory.

- **Public territory**, which includes non-reserved parking spaces, theatre seats, and restaurant tables, is open to everyone and is not held permanently by any individual.

- **Home territory** is a public space that is taken over, more or less continuously, by a group who feels as comfortable there as they would at home. If a group of friends meets at the same bar every evening, that establishment would be considered home territory for them.

- **Interactional territory** is a temporary space formed when people gather to converse. If a small group of individuals form a conversation circle at a party, others usually respect that area.

Territorial Defense

Animals mark territory; so do humans. Animals defend their space against encroachment; so do humans. First, we take preventative measures to discourage others from encroaching on our area. We may leave personal items to dissuade others from taking our space (like placing a coat on a theatre seat while we go buy popcorn), hang signs (like "no trespassing"), or simply try to look imposing so that others will not approach our territory (a library patron may spread papers and books across a table so that he will not be asked to share). Next, if someone does violate our territory, by using it or even trying to take it over, we react. We may place additional personal items or communiques in the area or go so far as to verbally or physically remove the intruder.

Haptics

Joseph A. DeVito of the City University of New York says, "Developmentally, touch is probably the first sense to be used. Even in the womb the fetus is stimulated by touch. Soon after birth the infant is fondled, caressed, patted, and stroked. In turn, the baby explores its world through touch" (179). In fact, throughout our lives, touching communication, or haptics, is a powerful tool.

Touch and Human Development

As DeVito implies, touch is essential to children's well being and even their survival. After World War II, the death rate of babies in European orphanages was extremely high even though the babies were safe and well fed. The reason? Because there were few workers to care for the children, they received almost no affectionate touch. When older women were hired to rock, feed, and hold the babies, the death rate dropped to almost zero. Also, the women, many of whom were widowed and childless, fared better than they had before they worked with the children.

As we grow, however, we give and receive touch less and less. Adolescents engage in about half as much physical contact as younger children, and adults touch even less. Desmond Morris believes that this lack of contact frustrates us, causing many people to resort to "licensed touchers" (129-32) (such as massage therapists and hair dressers), petting animals, and self-touch (rubbing your neck to relieve stress). Senior citizens receive less physical contact than any other group, which often contributes to feelings of isolation and loneliness among that age group.

Types of Touch

We touch differently depending on the circumstance. Following are different categories of touch:

- **Ritualistic touch** is primarily used for greetings and departures. Hand shaking, hugging, or putting your arm around someone's shoulders can all be used as ritualistic touch.

- **Task-related touch** is impersonal touch used to accomplish a purpose. It can be either professional-functional, which is business-like touch used by people such as doctors, hair stylists, and manicurists, or more simple behaviors, such as removing a piece of lint from a friend's face.

- **Positive affect touch** occurs between people who are in a close interpersonal relationship and is used to communicate positive emotions such as support, appreciation, inclusion, affection, or sexual interest.

- **Playful touch** is primarily used to decrease tension and lighten an interaction. For instance, when a friend is upset, you might punch him lightly on the arm.

- **Control touch** is used to communicate dominance. In our society, a person of higher status is typically more free to touch a subordinate than the other way around. A teacher might put his arm around a student when helping the child with a problem, for example.

Variance in Touch

A number of factors affect how we use touch. The first is gender. In general, women are more touch-oriented than men. Culture also affects our haptic behavior. In some countries, touching is much more accepted than in America. In the Middle East, for instance, it is not uncommon for two men to hold hands or link arms as they walk. In America, such behavior would be regarded dubiously. The final factor affecting the way we use physical contact is personality. Most likely, you have some friends who easily give hugs and seem to touch others constantly. On the other hand, some people grow uncomfortable when someone else touches them. "Touch avoidance" is the term used to refer to people who tend to resist touch. Interestingly, touch avoidance is linked to other communicative behaviors as it positively correlates with communication apprehension and negatively correlates with self-disclosure. In other words, people who avoid touch tend to be more shy and less likely to reveal themselves than those who use physical contact more frequently.

Paralanguage

Sounds, such as gasps and groans, and vocal qualities, like volume, pitch, resonance, rate, inflection, and tone, are considered paralanguage. Whether we use paralanguage intentionally or unintentionally, it reveals a great deal about what we really mean. Vocal cues tell how our statements should be interpreted (as a joke, a threat, a fact, a question, etc.), communicate feelings to others, and reveal our emotions. Paralanguage also affects how others perceive us. This is why we try to sound confident in a job interview, solemn when delivering a eulogy, and apologetic when seeking forgiveness. No matter what we say, we will be seen as inappropriate if we don't have the right tone.

The Elements of Paralanguage

- **Pitch.** If you tighten your vocal cords, the pitch of your voice will go up, while relaxed vocal cords cause your pitch to go down. Thus, intense feelings like anger, excitement, and fear cause a higher pitch while tiredness, depression, or simply a relaxed mood can make pitch lower. Further, if you have ever listened to a speaker who was excessively monotone, you know that such a speaking style can be dull and uninteresting. Try for variations in pitch when you speak to convey enthusiasm and to hold the attention of your listeners.

- **Resonance.** The richness or thinness of your voice also affects how you are perceived by others. Low, deep tones are seen as firm and self-assured while thin, high-pitched voices suggest timidity, insecurity, and weakness.

- **Articulation.** Formality can affect how clearly we enunciate our words. In a formal situation, such as a business meeting, we are more likely to speak clearly and precisely, while a drawl or slurred speech is more appropriate for informal discussions. It is unlikely that the guys in the beer commercial who greet each other by saying, "Whazzzzup?" would speak that way to their bosses. In general, good articulation is preferred as mumbling is associated with a lack of intelligence and competence.

- **Rate.** A fast tempo often reveals excitement or nervousness, while speech that is unusually slow communicates indifference. Studies indicate that a rate of 140-160 words a minute is ideal.

- **Volume.** Whether you use a loud voice or a soft one, volume can be a double-edged sword. Loud volume, on one hand, can communicate confidence, enthusiasm, and charisma. However, it can also be seen as overly aggressive. A soft voice can reveal caring, trustworthiness, and confidence but can also be perceived as showing a lack of assurance. Of course, what is appropriate in terms of volume is relative depending on the environment and situation. A teacher, for instance, would use a louder volume when speaking to a class in a large lecture hall than in a small classroom.

- **Rhythm.** By emphasizing different words in a sentence, a speaker can completely change the meaning of that sentence. Consider how different intonations alter the following statement:
  Do *I* want to go?
  Do I want to go!
  By emphasizing a different word, a speaker can change a sentence from a question of clarification to an excited declarative statement.

- **Pause and Silence.** Richmond and McCroskey note that, "Contrary to what many believe, silence is not the opposite of speaking. Silence should not be equated with not communicating" (110). Instead, silence can speak volumes. We use silence when we need to gather our thoughts, to show contentment with another person (such as two lovers enjoying a silent moment), to distance ourselves from others (the "silent treatment"), to allow an important point or a joke to be understood, and to show respect. When you speak, try to use pause and silence to your benefit. Apply effective pauses, which call attention to particular ideas, and avoid awkward pauses, where you use fillers like "uh," and "you know," which show that you are grasping for ideas.

Voice Printing

Undoubtedly, there are people you can identify simply by hearing their voices. When they call on the phone, you greet them by name even before they identify themselves. Because each of us has a unique voice, voice printing is a developing technology. Such technology has tremendous applications in the field of security. Eventually, when we go to the ATM, we may not need to remember a PIN. Simply speaking into the cash machine would suffice. According to Bob Zurek, senior analyst at Forrester Research, "Such a system might ask you to speak, and then your voice is recorded and stored in a database. The system also stores a challenging voice and the two are compared each time you enter the system, so it can positively identify you" (Gallagher).

Environment

Recently, there has been a surge of interest in Feng Shui (pronouned fung shway), a 4000-year-old Chinese philosophy that is believed to increase wealth, improve health, and promote rewarding relationships through the creation of harmonious, balanced working and living areas ("Feng Shui?"). Many people pay Feng Shui consultants thousands of dollars to rearrange their homes so that the energy, or "chi," in the environment works to their benefit. Whether or not you believe Feng Shui has merit, its underlying principle — that environment affects how people feel and interact — is indisputable.

Restaurants understand this principle. Upscale restaurants often use dim lights, comfortable chairs, soft music, and classy accouterments to make people feel more comfortable. Fast food restaurants, on the other hand, have hard plastic booths and bright lighting to encourage patrons to eat quickly and move on so that others may eat. Studies have found that background music can actually affect the rate at which people eat. When slow music is played, people eat 3.2 mouthfuls a minute, but when fast music is played, people eat as much as 5.1 mouthfuls a minute (Wood, 117).

Architecture

Winston Churchill once said, "We shape our buildings, thereafter they shape us." A new shopping mall in the Denver area is designed to look like a ski lodge. It uses wood extensively, is decorated in warm colors, and has numerous areas where customers can sit in soft, comfortable chairs next to fireplaces. The purpose of this design is to make customers feel comfortable, leading them to stay longer and consequently spend more money.

Courtrooms offer a perfect example of how architecture can be used to influence behavior. Almost invariably, they are decorated formally. Chairs and tables have permanence; specific areas are reserved for witnesses, the attorneys, the recorder, and the jury. Invariably, the judge's bench is elevated. Such design encourages respectful behavior and makes us aware of the seriousness of decisions that are made in the courtroom.

Seating Arrangements

If the legend of King Arthur is true, he was a student of nonverbal communication. According to the legend, King Arthur and his knights met at a round table so that all would be equal. Because there was no "head" of the table, everyone had the same status. Even today, this rings true. Round and square tables are used to communicate equality (though the sharp corners on a square table do not foster unity), while rectangular tables can suggest power for people seated at the short ends.

Another example that demonstrates how seating arrangements can affect interaction can be found in the classic film *It's a Wonderful Life*. At one point, George Bailey (played by Jimmy Stewart) goes to visit his rival Mr. Potter (Lionel Barrymore) in Potter's office. George is asked to sit down, and when he does, he sinks so low in the chair it is as if Potter towers over him. This was obviously a "power play" on Potter's part, designed to make anyone who came to his office feel inferior.

In fact, there are many ways offices can be arranged to communicate power. In business, there is much lore behind the "corner office," because the owner of that prime spot is considered important. Additionally, higher status individuals generally have offices that are more difficult to reach. When I was in high school, I was once summoned to the principal's office. To see him, I had to go through a waiting room and the secretary's office. Finally, like Mr. Potter, many people arrange the furniture in their office to convey power. The classic example of this is using the desk as a barrier by placing it between the occupant of the office and the door. In fact, many large offices are divided into two distinct areas: a pressure area, in which the desk is used to block the occupant from visitors, and the semisocial area, which is likely to have chairs arranged in a more conversational configuration without barriers. Negotiation and bargaining usually take place in the pressure area while informal discussion occurs in the semisocial area.

Color

In one study, three schools were studied over a period of two years. One was left unpainted, one was painted in neutral, institutional colors (buff walls and white ceilings), one was painted with bright, cheerful colors. After two years, the students who showed the greatest improvement in social skills and academic performance were those in the brightly painted school. Those in the unpainted school showed the least improvement (Richmond and McCroskey, 184-86). In fact, numerous studies indicate that colors can even affect vision, hearing, respiration, and circulation.

It has long been believed that the color pink could soothe aggressive behavior. Says Dr. Alexander Schauss, Ph.D., director of the American Institute for Biosocial Research in Tacoma, Washington, "Even if a person tries to be angry or aggressive in the presence of pink, he can't. The heart muscles can't race fast enough. It's a tranquilizing color that saps your energy" (Wu). Because of Dr. Schauss' research, pink is often used to calm violent prisoners in jail. Some sports teams have gone so far as to paint the opposing team's locker room pink in their stadium or arena with the hope that it will make the players passive. Because of this, the Western Athletic Conference now has a rule that both locker rooms must be painted the same color.

Temperature

If you've ever been to Arizona in the summer or Minnesota in the winter, you won't be surprised to discover that temperature affects our attitudes and productiveness. However, if you long to live in a place that is warm year-round, you might be surprised to learn that may not be best for you. First, people tend to accomplish more when the weather is not too hot. In his book, *The Achieving Society*, David C. McClelland reports that achievement motivation is greatest in societies where the average yearly temperature is between forty- and sixty-degrees Fahrenheit. People seem to do their best work in late winter, early spring, and fall. In addition to making us less productive, warm weather can cause us to be more hostile. In one study, researchers found that attitudes toward a hypothetical stranger were affected by the temperature. Subjects in a room heated to ninety-three degrees Fahrenheit had less positive reactions toward the stranger than subjects in a room at seventy-three degrees.

Chronemics

Chronemics is how we perceive and use time to define identities and relationships. Time is very important to us. We complain that "there is never enough time in a day," are upset when someone "wastes our time," and believe that "time is money." Because of this, the way we use time is very meaningful. Think about it this way: The way we spend our money tells a lot about us. It reveals our priorities, our outlook on life, and our social status. Our spending habits even show who is most important to us. If we really believe, then, that time *is* money, the way we use time can reveal many of the same things.

Time and Status

Status is conveyed very clearly through chronemics. It is more acceptable for people of high status to be late and to make others wait for them. When you go to the doctor, you almost always have to wait, even when you have an appointment. This sends the message that the doctor's time is more valuable than yours. Teachers can come late to class but students can't. Employees are often reprimanded for arriving to a meeting after it starts, but no one says a word if the boss comes in after the appointed time.

Psychological Time Orientation

Psychological time orientation is how people perceive time. This framework affects how we live and communicate on a daily basis. There seem to be three psychological orientations to time:

- **Past-oriented people** tend to focus on the past. If your grandfather constantly starts stories with, "In my day ..." he probably has a past-oriented framework. These people apply past events when seeking solutions for current problems.

- **Present-oriented people** live for today. They value the opinions of older people less than past-oriented people and make decisions based on immediate need and satisfaction.

- **Future-oriented people** work for tomorrow, basing decisions on the future. Such individuals are more likely to save and invest or work to alleviate future problems.

Consider these orientations within a marriage. When faced with monetary concerns, a past-oriented spouse might say, "We had a similar problem two years ago and were able to solve it. Let's try the same solution we used then." A present-oriented person might say, "It's OK. We need to have fun and the future will take care of itself." A future-oriented spouse might suggest, "We need to determine priorities so that we know how much we need to save." As you might expect, conflicts can arise when two people with different time orientations try to accomplish a common goal. But understanding these frameworks helps us to understand ourselves and others better, hopefully enabling us to work together more effectively.

Artifacts

Yet another way we communicate is through personal objects, such as clothing, jewelry, eyeglasses, or even a pen or pencil. First, artifacts announce professional identity. Military personnel wear uniforms to show the branch they serve and their rank. Professionals wear business suits. Fast food workers wear prescribed shirts and caps. Students wear jeans and carry backpacks.

Status is also revealed through artifacts. Some people wear

designer labels and expensive jewelry to show they have a great deal of money, while someone in worn, shoddy clothing will be perceived to be lower class. Legible clothing (anything you wear with a message that can be read) also communicates lower status and lack of power, according to author John Molloy. Though these impressions can sometimes be wrong, we persist in forming them.

Finally, we reveal our personalities through our dress and other artifacts. Our clothing shows whether we are conservative or liberal, our creativity, our sense of style, how committed we are to a job or a relationship, and to what degree we conform to society's standards. In one study, college students were shown pictures of a teacher dressed in informal and in more formal clothing. When the instructor was dressed informally, the students perceived her as friendly, fair, enthusiastic, and helpful. Dressed in conservative clothing, she was seen as prepared, knowledgeable, and organized. Younger students associated formal attire in teachers with disciplinary skills.

The Impact of a Hat

One of the most famous meetings between world leaders took place at the Geneva Summit of 1985 when Ronald Reagan and Russian premiere Mikhail Gorbachev first met. Though the landmark meeting was considered a success, Gorbachev and his aides later revealed that they were extremely annoyed to find Reagan waiting to meet them without a hat. Gorbachev, dressed for the cold weather in a thick gabardine coat and a winter hat, felt out of place and at a disadvantage to his American counterpart. According to the BBC, Gorbachev's wife Raisa later complained, "We Russians had no image makers, no one to advise us how to match up to the Americans" ("Getting to Know ..."). Reagan used other nonverbals to his advantage, as well. He waited for Gorbachev on the steps so that, when the Russian leader approached, Reagan would tower over him. As they walked up the steps, Reagan intentionally touched Gorbachev on the arm, as if the American president was helping the younger man up the steps. Clearly, one reason Reagan was nicknamed "The Great Communicator" was his understanding of the power of nonverbal communication.

Appearance

Height

Ronald Reagan is not the only politician who has manipulated nonverbals to his benefit. Before presidential debates, it is not uncommon for the handlers of the candidates to clash over seating and standing arrangements. They (and their image consultants) understand that, in our society, we associate height with power and dominance. Says Jay Matthews of the *Washington Post*, "The best measure of electability is the distance from the bottom of a candidate's calloused heels to the top of his or her well-coifed head ... We are a species that equates larger size with maturity, leadership, and sex appeal." Matthews reports that, in the thirteen presidential debates of the televised era, the shorter candidate has only won three times. Further, taking a random election year (1990), Matthews found that of the thirty-one contested U.S. Senate races, the shorter candidate won only eight.

This phenomenon led to the famed belt-buckle compromise of 1976. Because Jimmy Carter's handlers realized that the Democratic nominee was at a disadvantage to his taller opponent, Gerald Ford, they insisted that the candidates appear the same height during the debates. Consequently, the distance from Carter's and Ford's belt buckles to their podiums was adjusted so that they would each have equal torso exposure. Carter's people took additional steps, such as shooting him in campaign ads from a low angle, to make their candidate look taller. These measures apparently worked as Jimmy Carter was successful in bucking the height trend, defeating Gerald Ford in the 1976 election.

Attractiveness

There can be no debating the fact that, as a culture, we are obsessed with appearance. Look at all we do to conform to societal standards of attractiveness. Billions of dollars are spent each year on liposuction, breast implants, face lifts, manicures, pedicures, hair styles, and the "right" clothes. We go on diets and literally spend hours each day grooming and preening ourselves. Studies prove that this attitude affects the way we perceive others.

Attractive people are more likely to be considered successful, happy, sexually active, sensitive, competent, and responsive. In the workplace, people considered physically attractive are more likely to be hired, promoted, given opportunities for education and professional growth, and less likely to be fired.

Attractiveness even influences the way children are treated at school. Researchers have found many interesting (and somewhat disturbing) correlations between attractiveness and student-teacher interaction. Studies show that attractive students receive higher grades and more interaction from both their teachers and their classmates (Richmond and McCroskey, 25). Of course, such actions on the part of teachers are not intentional or malicious. Instead, they are the result of cultural stereotypes and expectations. Hopefully, studies that demonstrate such tendencies will make more instructors aware of such behavior so that it can be remedied.

Body Shape
There are three general body types:

- The **endomorph** has a rounded, oval-shaped body. People with this body type are usually heavy and sometimes described as "pear-shaped."

- The **ectomorph** is characterized as thin and bony, with an underdeveloped muscular tone.

- The **mesomorph** has a triangular body shape with broad shoulders and a narrow waist. Firm, muscular, and athletic-looking, mesomorphs have a shape that most people desire.

As you've probably guessed, we also draw conclusions about people based on their body shape. Endomorphs are seen as slow, sociable, emotional, and relaxed. Ectomorphs are considered to be tense, meticulous, and detached. Mesomorphs are perceived as confident and energetic, but also dominant and hot-tempered. Many famous and fictitious characters fit these stereotypes. Santa Claus (an endomorph) is jolly. Homer Simpson (an endomorph) is much more relaxed — lazy, even — than his wife Marge (a mesomorph).

In this case, however, such assumptions may be more than

generalization and stereotyping. Researcher William Sheldon, among others, has found that there seems to be a correlation between body shape and the aforementioned personality traits. This brings up an unresolvable "chicken and egg" argument. Are such perceptions caused by people's behavior, or do we create self-fulfilling prophecies by treating people according to our expectations?

Improving Nonverbal Communcation Skills

So, is the field of nonverbal communication nothing more than a collection of fascinating facts and trivia tidbits concerning the way we communicate? Absolutely not! Given that nonverbals are such a potent communicative tool it makes sense that if we improve the way we use and read nonverbal signals, we will be better communicators. You've already completed the first step by reading this chapter: developing an awareness of nonverbal cues and behaviors. Now you are more equipped to evaluate your nonverbals to see if they compliment what you are saying and can also determine if you are sending messages you don't want others to see. You can also interpret the nonverbals of others so that you can understand and empathize with them more deeply.

Also, remember to strive for congruence. Have you ever asked a date if they would like to see a certain movie and had that person reply, "Sure, why not?" in an uninterested tone of voice? Chances are, you weren't sure whether you should go ahead and purchase tickets for that film or suggest a different one. Make your verbal and nonverbal signals match. This will help others discern your true feelings.

Finally, remember that nonverbal communication varies from person to person. You cannot tell what another person is thinking just by looking at them. While a knowledge of the principles of nonverbal communication can certainly help us understand others better, all nonverbal cues must be interpreted according to context.

Conclusion

There is an old country song that says, "You say it best when you say nothing at all." Because so much of what we communicate is done with nonverbals, we really do communicate best when we "say nothing at all."

Chapter Five

Managing Conflict

Gangster Al Capone is reported to have said, "You can get a lot more with a smile and a gun than with just a smile." However, if you're not willing to become a gangster or spend the rest of your life in prison, you might want to find a more productive way to resolve conflict. This chapter will help you understand the nature of conflict and develop strategies for resolving disputes constructively.

What Is Conflict?

Conflict exists when two individuals or groups who depend on each other have different views, needs, interests, or perspectives. Conflicts may be small, like two friends arguing over which restaurant to patronize, or as large as a war between nations. Because the focus of this book is on interpersonal relationships, this chapter will focus on conflicts between individuals. Conflict is not a sign that a relationship is in trouble, but the way people deal with their problems is a measure of relationship health. That is, conflicts exist in even the best relationships. It's just that the individuals in healthy relationships deal with their problems well.

Conflict Is Inevitable

Everyone constantly copes with conflict. No matter where you are — at work, at school, at home, or on the street — you will inevitably encounter conflict. And no matter who you are — a professional, a student, a sales clerk, a husband, wife, son, or daughter — you will inevitably benefit from learning strategies to deal with that conflict.

Conflict May Be Overt or Covert

Overt conflict exists when people openly acknowledge problems and differences and deal with them in a direct, honest manner. In this case, the problem is defined and discussed as both parties honestly state their needs and points of view. Unfortunately, we too often engage in covert conflict by indirectly expressing our anger or dissatisfaction. A husband who is upset with his wife may, instead of directly discussing the source of his anger, become cold and distant toward her. Such "game playing" makes it almost impossible to resolve conflicts.

Conflict May Focus on Content or the Relationship

Content conflict centers on issues that are external to the parties involved. What movie to watch, the quality of a song or a band, and the merits of a particular make of car are all conflicts that center on content. Relationship conflicts focus more on the individuals involved and not the issues. Who is in charge of a project at work, whether a boss is treating you fairly, and whether your parents are favoring one of your siblings are all examples of this type of conflict.

Interestingly, relationship conflicts are often hidden and manifest themselves as content conflicts. For instance, two roommates may be arguing over which television show to watch, but the real issue is that one individual feels that the other selfishly exerts too much control over the TV. It can help you to realize this so that when it seems you are arguing over some trivial subject, you can refocus discussion on to the real issue and have a better chance of solving that problem.

Conflict: The Good, the Bad, and the Ugly

The Chinese word for conflict is made up of two characters: one for "danger," the other for "opportunity." This is insightful, because when conflict is not handled well, it can be an extremely dangerous element in a relationship. On the other hand, conflict affords us the opportunity to resolve problems and strengthen our relationships if we know how to deal with it.

The Downside of Conflict

Though conflict is unavoidable, almost no one enjoys it. Further, if it is handled poorly, conflict can hurt relationships. First, according to Joseph A. DeVito, conflict almost always leads to increased negative regard for the opponent and, as DeVito says, "When this opponent is someone you love or care for very deeply, it can create serious problems for the relationship" (279). Also, conflict can sap energy that would be better spent on other areas, like resolving the issue. When I was young, my parents would sometimes tell me that if I spent as much time doing my chores as I spent complaining about them, I could have been done much sooner. Finally, in the worst case, unresolved conflicts can cause individuals to close themselves off to one another and can end relationships. The consequences of this can range from the fairly insignificant (a potential car buyer storming out of the dealership because of what he perceives as unfair treatment) to the very significant (a marriage ending in divorce because of what is legally termed "irreconcilable differences").

The Upside of Conflict

The good news, however, is that conflict doesn't have to be hurtful or harmful to relationships. If effective conflict management strategies are used, disputes can actually be good for individuals and relationships. First, conflict can be beneficial because it can help you get what you want. Let's face it: The only way to have your needs and desires fulfilled is to state them. Telling others what you want sometimes creates conflict. So, it is often necessary to deal with conflict in order to have your needs met.

Conflict can help you understand others better. A fight with a boyfriend or girlfriend can enable you to know more about your significant other and can make your relationship stronger. Conflict also prevents hostilities and resentments from festering, which can lead to larger problems down the road. Further, conflict forces you to consider other points of view, opening your mind to new ideas. A final benefit of conflict is that it demonstrates to the other person that the relationship is worth the effort. If you didn't care about the other person, you would simply walk away when faced with a problem. If you're fighting, the relationship must be worth fighting for.

Views of Conflict

No doubt you've heard the expression "win-win." Sports teams use it when they make a trade to indicate that both teams will benefit from the deal; salesmen use it when convincing you to buy something; bosses use it at meetings to sound smart. This expression comes from a theory of conflict management that states there are three different ways to view conflict: lose-lose, win-lose, and win-win. Different conflicts fall into different categories. The trick is to know which type of conflict we are engaged in so that we may respond to the conflict appropriately. Too often, though, we attempt to apply one philosophy to all conflicts.

Lose-Lose

This approach to conflict assumes that conflict results in losses for everyone involved. People who have this philosophy tend to avoid conflict since they believe no good can come of it. This causes a self-fulfilling prophecy. By refusing to engage in conflict, people with this orientation ensure they never solve interpersonal problems and do indeed create a lose-lose situation.

Win-Lose

This philosophy asserts that, in a disagreement, one party involved will win and the other will lose. People who follow this orientation believe that, much like in sports, only one person can get what they want as the result of a conflict. For instance, one carpooler might like to listen to hard rock on the radio while his partner prefers smooth jazz. If they have a win-lose approach to conflict, they will see only two possible options (the stations each prefers) and ignore other solutions. The problem with this approach is that one person has to lose, which causes resentment and, in the long run, hurts the relationship. Julia Wood says, "For this reason, win-lose orientations should really be called win-lose-lose because when one person wins, both the other person and the relationship can lose."

Win-Win

The healthiest approach to conflict management, the win-win orientation assumes that there are ways to resolve differences so that everyone benefits and feels good about the solution. This may be done through compromise or a unique solution that neither party had previously considered. For instance, there are many ways the carpoolers could resolve their debate over radio stations. They could take turns picking the station, find a third station that plays a more eclectic mix of music, or bring CDs to play instead of the radio. This approach works best because it takes into account the feelings and needs of everyone involved.

Nonproductive Strategies for Dealing with Conflict

Because many of us lack any training in conflict management, we develop ineffective and unhealthy ways to deal with disagreements. The first step in learning to effectively resolve conflicts is to recognize and avoid the following nonproductive strategies identified by Joseph A. DeVito (282-85):

Avoidance

When we avoid a conflict, we simply refuse to deal with it. We may physically flee the dispute by leaving the area or emotionally withdraw by refusing to discuss any of the issues raised or by giving the other person the silent treatment. Studies show that men use avoidance more than women and are also more likely to deny that any problem exists. Since an issue can't be resolved unless it is dealt with by both individuals involved, avoidance obviously blocks successful conflict management.

Physical Force

Sadly, too many people allow conflict to escalate to the point it becomes a physical fight. When this happens, the issues are completely ignored and it becomes impossible to resolve the conflict with a "win-win" result. Instead, both participants lose because the relationship is irreparably damaged. Even worse, physical force is used much too often in families and among people who love each other. In one study, it was discovered that seventy percent of divorced couples reported at least one episode of violence in their relationship.

Blame

A husband has a hard day at work and comes home in a grumpy mood. When he gets home, his wife tells him that she forgot to pick up the suit from the cleaners he needs for an important meeting. He snaps at her, calls her irresponsible, and accuses her of never doing anything to help him. She snaps back that he should have reminded her before he left for work. Who is to blame for this conflict?

Clearly, it is impossible to pin blame on one individual or one action. Both spouses contributed to the escalation of the argument.

However, it is common for us to try to blame our partner in conflict by asserting that it is all the other person's fault. If the couple in our example continue to blame each other for their problems, the husband's feelings that his wife doesn't do enough for him will go unaddressed and the relationship will be damaged.

Silencers

Silencers are any of a variety of fighting techniques that literally silence the other person. Perhaps the most common silencer is crying, which forces the other individual to forget the issue and console the person in tears. Consider this situation: A student asks the teacher if she can use the restroom. He tells her that she has taken too many passes lately and should remain in class. She begins to tear up while asserting that she has to deal with an important problem. What is the teacher to do? If he holds firm to his position, he runs the risk of causing the student distress. If he allows her to go, he is allowing her to miss important instruction. In either case, the issue of why this student leaves class so much is not discussed.

In addition to crying, other silencers include feigned emotionalism, yelling, and claiming symptoms (like pretending to have a headache). The problem with silencers is that the other individual can never be sure if the silencer is an authentic reaction or if it is being faked to manipulate the dispute. Does the student really have a problem to deal with or is she just using that as an excuse so that she can talk to a friend in the hall? Does the husband really have a headache or is he merely trying to avoid discussing a marital problem?

Gunnysacking

This technique involves storing up grievances (as if in a large gunnysack) rather than dealing with them as they arise, so that you may unload them all at once. All it takes is one small precipitating event for the gunnysacker to dump the whole bag of complaints. A teenager may come home after curfew, but instead of punishing him for this indiscretion, his father yells at him for his low grades, his rebellious manner of dress, and the fact that he never cleans his room. The problem with this approach is that gunnysacking fosters gunnysacking from the other person ("If you're going to list everything I've done to you, I'll recite everything you've done to me"), which builds resentment on both sides of the dispute.

Manipulation

My father is an expert manipulator. If he has a problem at a restaurant, a store, or the airport, he will become especially courteous toward the clerk. He will empathize with the employee's situation by saying things like, "I know you're doing all you can in a difficult situation," and "This isn't your fault at all — you're the only one here who seems to know what you're doing!" Through this charming and disarming behavior, my father gets clerks to do whatever he wants (and then some!). This technique works because it gets the other individual into a receptive and noncombative frame of mind and plays on the tendency people have to give in to people who are especially nice to them. While this strategy is not as harmful as other nonproductive means of dealing with conflict, it can still create problems. When one person simply gives in, a win-lose situation may be created (even if the loser doesn't feel like one) and the best solution may be ignored.

Personal Rejection

Instead of dealing with a conflict, some individuals withhold affection from their opponents until those individuals give in to their demands. When I was in college, I spent two summers working at a daycare. Though only six years old, one little girl had mastered this strategy. If her friends wouldn't play the game she wanted to play, she would tell them they weren't her friends anymore and leave them alone. Invariably, the threatened loss of friendship would be enough to cause the other girls to give in to the demands of their difficult friend. This technique is not just used by children, however. A boyfriend might break up with his girlfriend to get his way on an issue; a wife might withhold intimacy from her husband because he forgot her birthday.

Hitting Below the Belt

In boxing, it is against the rules to hit an opponent below his beltline as that would inflict serious pain. Like boxers, we all have a "beltline," or a personal limit of hurt or tolerance that we can bear. In most interpersonal relationships, we know where the other person's beltline is. We hit below the belt when we bring up an issue that is especially hurtful for the other person and inflict serious emotional pain.

Verbal Aggressiveness

Verbal aggressiveness is a method of winning an argument by damaging your opponent's self-concept through personal attacks. For instance, when debating the merits of a novel, you might say, "You're so stupid you wouldn't know good writing if it bit you on the nose!"

Fair Fighting: Productive Strategies for Dealing with Conflict

So now that you know what not to do when engaged in disputes with others, let's turn our attention to productive strategies for conflict resolution. If you follow these principles and avoid the harmful and hurtful strategies discussed above, you will become much better at finding win-win solutions to conflict, more successfully satisfy your needs as well as the needs of those close to you, and develop stronger interpersonal relationships.

Accept and Confirm Others

One trademark of the nonproductive approaches to conflict listed above is that they view the opponent as someone to defeat, or steamroll, as you attempt to win the dispute. In contrast, one characteristic of effective conflict management is concern for the other person involved. If you truly have their best interests at heart, you will work much harder to find mutually beneficial solutions to conflict.

Affirm and Assert Yourself

While you accept others, you must give them the chance to do the same for you. The only way to do so is to honestly communicate your thoughts and feelings and to let others know what you hope to gain from the solution to the conflict. Use the techniques of assertive communication described in Chapter Two of this text. Remember the defining characteristic of assertive communication is defending your legitimate rights without violating the legitimate rights of others.

Respect Diversity

Because people are all unique, our relationships with different individuals are also diverse. We cannot use the same strategies to solve problems or resolve conflicts with each person we encounter. You may have one coworker who is very straightforward and takes criticism well and another colleague who is much more sensitive. It is imperative that you find different ways to broach difficult subjects with these two individuals. Thus, adaptation is a key to success in interpersonal communication and particularly in conflict management.

Create a Supportive Climate

According to Tim Borchers of Moorhead State University, climate affects the success with which conflict is managed. Avoid a defensive climate, which is marked by critical evaluation, attempts to gain control, the use of hidden agendas, indifference to the problem, and stubbornness. Strive for a supportive climate, which is characterized by empathy, equality among participants, honesty, and active listening.

Show Grace

Julia Wood defines grace as "granting forgiveness or putting aside our needs or helping another save face when no standard says we should or must do so" (77). It can often be helpful to display grace when embroiled in conflict. If you forgive someone for wronging you (even if they don't ask for forgiveness), do a favor for someone when they neither ask nor expect you to do so, or defer to another person's preference instead of imposing your own, you are demonstrating grace. Wood points out that grace is not doing what you should (forgiving those who aren't responsible for their actions or giving in when you have no choice, like when your boss tells you to do something you don't want to do), nor is it anything that is done with the hope of receiving payback. Instead it is a gift, freely given without any expectation of reciprocity.

It is not always appropriate to show grace, nor should this contradict the principle of affirming and asserting yourself. If someone takes advantage of your kindness or exploits your showing of grace, you may not be so quick to demonstrate this quality a second time. Nor would it necessarily be wise to do so. If a parent forgives a teenager for smarting off, and the child takes advantage of that grace by continuing to speak in a disrespectful manner, the parent would only be opening himself to further abuse by continuing to show grace without asserting his own needs. Still, even though some people may take advantage, showing grace is noble, demonstrates your commitment to a relationship, and can often be a giant step toward reconciliation.

Fight in Private

When you argue in the presence of others, you run the risk of embarrassing yourself and the person you are debating, you may not be willing to be totally honest, and you are more likely to use nonproductive strategies because you feel you have to win to save face. The best way to resolve conflict is to find a quiet, private spot where you can discuss the issue in a calm, honest manner.

Pick a Good Time to Manage Conflict

Though conflict should be managed quickly to avoid gunnysacking, you sometimes need to postpone a discussion until you've found an appropriate location and both partners are emotionally ready and free from distraction. It is not best to pick a fight as your partner is rushing out the door late for work, or when he or she has just returned home from a hard day, or when emotions are high. Just be sure that you do set a definite time in the near future to resolve the conflict. Never say "now is not the time" simply to avoid dealing with an issue.

Know What You Are Fighting About

Remember the discussion of content conflict and relationship conflict at the beginning of this chapter? Be sure that you always define the problem when you manage conflict and that you are not using the content of an argument to express festering anger or resentment about relationship issues.

Also, when you argue, be specific and stick to the point. Don't say, "You're too rude," when you really mean, "It bothers me when you're late to dinner and I have to wait for you." And — if the issue really is your friend's punctuality — don't discuss how she also chews with her mouth open. If that bothers you, too, discuss it as a separate issue after you resolve the first problem.

Finally, don't drag groups, institutions, third parties, religions, or ideas into the debate. Keep your focus on the person with whom you have a problem. Comments like, "No one in management seems to care about us employees," or "We could have solved this had you not brought your sister into it" do nothing to help you work through your problems with any one individual.

Be Prepared

We rehearse if we have to make a speech or presentation; we study (well, some people, anyway) before a test; we practice before a sporting event. Why, then, do we try to resolve conflicts unprepared? It's not that they aren't important. The very survival of relationships depends on how well we manage them. Before your discussion, determine exactly what the issue is and think about your needs, the needs of your partner, and possible solutions.

Fight About Problems That Can Be Solved

Arguing about issues over which neither individual in the conflict has any control, like the behavior of family members or an irreversible set of circumstances, saps time and energy and solves nothing. Instead, if the real cause of the conflict is something that can be fixed, reframe the issue. If it isn't, empathic listening may be a more appropriate response.

Withhold Quick Retorts

Especially when the other party hits you below the belt or says something unkind, it is tempting to "put them in their place." However, doing so will often lead to escalation of the conflict and negative feelings. Before you respond to a hurtful statement, take a few seconds to calm down and decide if you will later regret what you are about to say and if it will help solve the dispute or lead to further conflict.

Summarize

When an issue has been thoroughly discussed and you are near resolution, take a few seconds to summarize. Go over the problem and the solutions that have been agreed upon, and tell how you feel about the process of conflict management that you have used. If the issue isn't resolved, go over the progress you have made, what still needs to be addressed, and when you plan to meet to deal with those unresolved issues. After debating spending habits with a spouse or roommate, you might say, "I really appreciate you discussing this issue with me. I think we understand how we each view finances now and I really like your idea to keep track of our spending habits so that we don't just waste money. I'd still like to figure out a way we can save for new furniture. Maybe we can discuss that tomorrow at dinner if you don't mind."

Dealing with People Who Won't Fight Fair

The suggestions above are great, as long as everyone involved in the conflict agrees to abide by them. But we all know that's not always going to happen. It's a sad fact of life that there will always be people who refuse to fight fair. You may know exactly what manipulative strategies they are using as a result of reading this chapter, but that's not always going to help you either. If you tell someone, "You are gunnysacking and I really think we need to create a supportive environment in which to manage conflict," you probably won't dispel their anger! With this in mind, the following are specific techniques to help you deal with people who won't use productive means to resolve conflict:

Consider Your Opponent's Interests

If the person you are in conflict with refuses to affirm you or see your point of view, look more closely at their needs and desires. If they are going to fight selfishly, appeal to that selfish nature. Figure out how your perspective could benefit them and present solutions that meet their needs. If your roommate refuses to contribute to the stereo you want to buy for the apartment, you could show him how he could use it at the party he's planning to give. If he's afraid you'll always use it to play the polka music you love and he hates, assure him that you'll use headphones whenever you listen to your music.

Reframe Personal Attacks as Attacks on the Problem

If an opponent in an argument attacks you personally, restate that attack as an attack on the problem. This will refocus discussion where it belongs: on the issue. If someone tells you that you're being "unreasonable," say to them, "I can see we both feel strongly about this issue, but I'm glad you are concerned with finding a reasonable solution. Can you suggest a compromise that would be beneficial for both of us?"

Use a Content to Process Shift

Since assertive communication is a key element of conflict resolution, many of the special assertive techniques described in Chapter Two can help you manage interpersonal conflict. One such technique is the content to process shift. As we've already mentioned, you may not want to use technical lingo such as "gunnysacking," but you can still move conversation away from the content of the conversation to the process of communication. Perhaps you could say, "Can we take a time-out for just a second? You seem to be dumping a lot of issues on me at once. We're not going to solve anything if we both bring up the past. Right now, we're trying to decide whose turn it is to mow the lawn. Can we stick to that?"

There will always be people who are unwilling to work toward resolution of a conflict. They may only be interested in having their way or they may even be using the conflict to achieve an unrelated purpose (a boyfriend may pick small fights with his girlfriend because he wants to break up but is afraid to say so). That doesn't mean it's not worth trying these techniques; in many situations and with many people, they will help you resolve problems.

Conclusion

William E. Channing, noted author and clergyman, said, "Difficulties are meant to rouse, not discourage. The human spirit is to grow strong by conflict." No matter how much you try to avoid it, you will have to deal with interpersonal conflict. However, that doesn't have to be a bad thing. Conflict can actually strengthen relationships, as long as you avoid manipulative and nonproductive techniques for resolving problems and apply productive conflict management strategies.

Chapter Six

Persuasion

Whether you realize it or not, you are constantly bombarded by persuasive messages. Commercials on television and the radio try to convince you to spend your money on their products; bumper stickers and billboards encourage you to feel a certain way; friends exert pressure to get you to do whatever it is they want you to do; teachers and bosses attempt to motivate you. You also use persuasion as you try to influence the behaviors of those around you. Convincing a friend to loan you money, asking a member of the opposite sex on a date, motivating your teammates to practice longer and harder, and teaching a child how to behave are all persuasive appeals you might make in a typical day.

Because persuasion is so omnipresent, it is a good idea for us to learn about this aspect of communication. This chapter will give you tools to deal with the multitude of persuasive appeals aimed at you and will also make you better at influencing others. After all, who doesn't want to become better at getting others to do what you want them to do? As Sharon Franklin and Deborah J. Clark point out in their book, *Essentials of Speech Communication*, persuasive skills can help you in the workplace as well as in daily life. They say, "Training in persuasive speaking techniques can help you to critique proposals, advance new project or product ideas, land new clients, change working conditions or company policies, sell services and products to others, and more" (172).

What Is Persuasion?

A message that attempts to influence people's opinions, attitudes, or actions is persuasion. The primary purpose of a persuasive appeal is to either change or reinforce attitudes and behaviors. While informative speakers are content to merely be understood, speakers who want to persuade must go further and convince their audience to do something. A candidate for public office speaking at a rally, a teenager seeking a later curfew, a public service announcement urging viewers not to drink and drive, and a motivational speech are all examples of persuasive messages.

Since persuasive appeals come in so many forms, the principles presented in this chapter apply to persuasion in general. Therefore, whether you are making a persuasive speech, convincing a friend to do something with you, or analyzing the merits of a lecture, advertisement, or personal appeal, you will be better equipped to deal with that situation competently.

Aristotle's Pathos, Logos, and Ethos

The most influential theory regarding persuasion was conceived in the fourth century B.C. by the Greek philosopher Aristotle. In his work *Rhetoric*, Aristotle provided instruction in speechmaking, dealing primarily with the art of persuasion. Aristotle identified three different types of proof that may be used by persuasive speakers: ethos, which are ethical and personal appeals emanating from the credibility of the source of the message; pathos, or emotional appeals; and logos, or logical appeals. Though a persuasive appeal may focus exclusively on one type of appeal, and it is rare for a message to have all three of these modes in equal amounts, the best persuasive messages strive to blend all three types of proof.

Pathos

Pathos, the first type of proof, is an appeal to the emotions of the audience. Perhaps the best way to change someone's attitude is to make them identify with or have strong feelings toward the topic. There is an old saying that, in love, "the heart rules the head." This is true — and not just in matters of love. As McCutcheon, Schaffer, and Wycoff note, "People would like to think that they make decisions based on reason. The truth is, however, that most people rely on their feelings as much as — or more than — their reason" (369). Because of this, persuasive speakers must make a conscious effort to make their message real for the audience.

Perhaps the best way to develop pathos is through the use of vivid illustration and example. Joseph Stalin once said, "One death is a tragedy; a million is a statistic." This means that when we just hear statistics, an issue may not seem real to us. But when a speaker can give the topic a human face, the listeners will be much more moved to action. Think about advertisements for charity. Do they simply tell how many children suffer from a certain disease? Of course not. Usually, they tell the story of one child who suffers and could benefit from your donation. By making us feel strongly for that individual, the charity is much more successful at fundraising.

Humor is also an effective emotional appeal. When persuasive speakers use humor, they break the tension and create positive feelings toward themselves and the issue. When Ronald Reagan was running for reelection for president in 1984, many were concerned about his advanced age (he was seventy-three years old). In one of the debates, Reagan was asked about this issue. Even though his opponent, Walter Mondale, was not exactly a spring chicken and had been Vice President of the United States, Reagan vowed, "I am not going to exploit, for political purposes, my opponent's youth and inexperience." With this one joke, Reagan put the age issue completely to rest (without really addressing the issue).

Too often, we rely solely on emotional appeals. Advertisements may appeal to our need for prestige (trying to get us to buy an expensive car or name brand clothing) without giving any logical reasons why their product is better than their competitor's. This may work for short periods of time with audiences who do not respond thoughtfully to messages. However, research indicates that pathos works best when it is combined with well reasoned logical arguments. This brings us to Aristotle's second component of persuasion ...

Logos

The Greek word logos means reason or logic and is the second necessary component of a persuasive message. This aspect of an effective appeal satisfies the analytical needs of the audience. Even though they may be moved by pathos, listeners also need to know that an argument makes sense; that is, it must follow the rules of logic and be verifiable. Consider the example of the charity above.

While the use of a child as an example may move the audience and make them receptive to helping, they also want to know that their money won't be wasted. Therefore, charities also show the advances that are being made in research and how donations will be used so potential donors know their money will actually help the children who need it.

The two best ways to develop logic in a persuasive appeal are through the use of organization and reason. Studies show that, because audiences can follow well structured messages more easily, they are more likely to be persuaded by them. Specific patterns for organizing persuasive messages will be presented later in this chapter. Secondly, the use of research and evidence demonstrates that you have done your homework and that there are experts in the field who agree with you. Statistics, facts, quotations, and stories taken from books, articles, and news reports can all add logos to your attempts to persuade others. If I wrote this book entirely from my own experience, you probably wouldn't have much faith in the information presented. What if your experience doesn't fit mine? But, through the use of research, I can show universal trends in human communication identified by others who have studied this subject in great depth. Hopefully, this will make the information I present more believable.

Ethos

Perhaps the most overlooked component of persuasion, but quite likely the most important, ethos is the ethics, or believability, of the speaker. Also called source credibility, this aspect does not refer as much to something a speaker says as who he or she is. If a friend recommends someone as a potential employee, you may hire that person because of your trust in your friend. If a successful stockbroker tells you to invest in a certain company, you buy stock because of his word. In both of these cases, you are being persuaded by the credibility of the source of a persuasive message.

Source credibility actually exists in the mind of the listener and is not an actual characteristic of a speaker. Supporters of a politician might have faith in his proposals while members of the opposing party will automatically be skeptical of any plan he presents. Even so, there are steps you can take to build your ethos. Following are the elements of source credibility:

- **Competency.** The first way to build credibility is to prove yourself an expert on the subject you are discussing. This may be done through the use of research, which shows that you have taken the time to study the subject, and by referring to your experience with the subject. Shortly before he died of lung cancer, actor Yul Brenner did a series of commercials urging viewers to avoid cigarettes. Since he had already received a death sentence from his lifelong smoking habit, he had more credibility than someone who had never smoked and could only speak in theoretical terms.

- **Trustworthiness.** If a speaker has a reputation for dishonesty, it is unlikely that an audience will believe anything he says. Why should they? If he has lied in the past, it's likely he will lie again. It's like the story of the boy who cried wolf. Because he lied twice, no one came to his rescue when he yelled for help a third time. Like this boy, you will be eaten alive if you compromise your honesty. You can also develop trustworthiness by demonstrating sincerity and genuine concern for your listeners. Further, studies show that we are more likely to believe someone who is like us. This is why candidates for public office often try to portray themselves as "Regular Joes and Janes." We're unlikely to vote for someone who we believe can't understand the problems we face in our daily lives.

- **Dynamism.** Franklin and Clark say, "Enthusiasm is contagious. If you are excited about and sincerely believe in the ideas you're presenting, it is likely that the audience will be also" (180). This is the component of source credibility that is most under your control because you can adjust your delivery style to reflect excitement and an upbeat attitude.

- **Goodwill.** If you have the best interests of your listeners at heart, they will be more receptive to your message. You can demonstrate concern for your audience by tailoring your message to fit their specific needs and interests (if speaking to a group of high school students, don't talk about retirement planning), complimenting them, and listening carefully when others speak.

Using Pathos, Logos, and Ethos

If you want to be persuasive, strive to blend pathos, logos, and ethos when you speak. You must consider each of these elements and make sure they are all present in your message. I once heard a speech on the subject of choosing a college. The speaker provided great logical support, citing graduation rates, tuition costs, and the relative strength of academic programs. However, he quickly lost the attention of the audience. Why? He did not connect to them in any way. Despite the high level of logic, the presentation had almost no emotional appeal and the speaker had no credibility with his audience.

In contrast, I also had the opportunity to hear Tom Sutherland, a college professor who was held hostage in Lebanon for six-and-one-half years. His experiences, his sense of humor, and his intelligence gave him instant credibility. His insightful analysis of the political environment that led to his capture demonstrated logic, while his detailed descriptions of his suffering provided potent emotional appeals. Dr. Sutherland was a speaker who effectively blended all three of Aristotle's persuasive components.

Other Views of Persuasion

Though the most influential theory of persuasion, Aristotle's perspective is not the only view of how we are influenced by others. Two other theories, Cognitive Dissonance and Maslow's Hierarchy of Needs, also shed light on what motivates us to alter our beliefs and actions.

Cognitive Dissonance

Cognitive Dissonance Theory states that two or more beliefs can either be in consonance (consistent) or dissonance (inconsistent), but that inconsistency is psychologically uncomfortable, so we strive for consonance. Thus, when we hold two contradictory beliefs, we are motivated to change one. This is when persuasion occurs.

Cognitive Dissonance Theory can best be explained through an example. Let's say an older man holds the opinion that all teenagers are troublemakers. Then a family moves in next door. The sixteen-year-old girl in the family befriends the man, frequently stopping to talk with him and even volunteering to help with household chores. His view of the girl now contradicts his view of teenagers in general. According to dissonance theory, he will now be motivated to rethink his view of teenagers (maybe they're not all bad after all) or the girl (she must want something from me).

Using this theory, you need to create dissonance in the minds of your listeners if you want to make them susceptible to persuasion. Determine their core beliefs and offer evidence that contradicts those beliefs. Once they are confronted with contradictory information, they will feel the need to resolve that dissonance, hopefully by adopting your ideas. Later, we will discuss Monroe's Motivated Sequence, an organizational format for persuasive appeals that uses the principle of cognitive dissonance.

Maslow's Hierarchy of Needs

Another theory that explains how humans are motivated was conceived by theorist Abraham Maslow. This theory holds that humans act to satisfy basic needs — physical needs, safety needs, social needs, ego needs, and self needs — and that we must meet them in ascending order. That is, unless we have satisfied our basic physical needs, we cannot even think of satisfying higher needs. In the order they must be attained, here is a closer look at the basic human needs identified by Maslow:

- **Physical needs** are food, air, water, clothing, shelter, and health. These must be realized first and foremost.

- **Safety needs** reflect our concerns for physical security. Once we have satisfied our physical needs, we think about how we can remain safe and free from harm.

- **Social needs.** Next, people focus on their longing for love, friendship, and inclusion.

- **Ego needs**, or our desire for self-esteem and self-respect, come next. If we feel comfortable, safe, and accepted, we begin to look inward to achieve peace with ourselves.

- **Self needs.** The highest need that humans strive to satisfy is the desire to be self-actualized, which is the feeling that you have reached your highest potential and achieved all that you are capable of achieving.

So how can this theory help you when you attempt to influence others through persuasion? First, you must be aware of your audience and satisfy their needs, both in reality and in your message. Why do you think so many motivational speakers provide donuts and coffee to their audience? It is because they realize that unless the audience is fed and comfortable they will not be receptive to any message.

Also, you can tailor your message to these needs. Show your audience how your proposals can satisfy the basic human needs. For instance, a politician might tell an audience that his platform will provide clean air and water (physical needs), reduce crime (safety needs), allow them more leisure time to spend with family and friends (social needs), make them more self-reliant (ego needs), and help them to achieve their dreams (self needs). Advertisers use Maslow's Hierarchy as well. We are told to eat a candy bar to satisfy our hunger (physical needs), buy a home security system (safety needs), purchase clothing that will attract the opposite sex (social needs), drive a prestigious, expensive car (ego needs), and to find a more satisfying job online (self needs). Really, Maslow's ideas help you to know your audience better. If you understand how they are motivated, you'll be better at appealing to their needs and desires.

Adapting Persuasion to Your Audience

When you were a young child, you probably knew how to influence your parents. When asking for a new toy, you modified your message depending on who you were asking. With your mom, you might have been sure to say "please," while a forlorn expression and a big hug may have been the best way to manipulate your dad. Likewise, the first step when attempting to influence others, especially if you are making a persuasive speech, is to know whom you're addressing. There are four basic types of audiences you will encounter: supportive, neutral, apathetic, and opposed audiences.

The Supportive Audience

This type of audience is friendly. Its members like you and support your position. A football coach addressing his own student body at a pep rally, a minister speaking before his congregation, and a civil rights leader encouraging a minority group would all be in front of supportive audiences. Because this type of audience is predisposed to your position, you don't need to spend a lot of time arguing your points or providing information. Instead, use your message to reinforce your listeners' beliefs, to deepen their commitment to the cause, and to energize them to action. Pathos can be of great use with a supportive audience as emotional appeals can excite and enthuse the listeners.

The Neutral Audience

People in a neutral audience may be interested in the subject you are discussing, but they don't have enough information about that issue to have formulated an opinion. An employer interviewing candidates for a job and a jury hearing arguments in a trial would be considered neutral because they start with little information and because they are committed to remaining unbiased. With a neutral audience, you must make your presentation interesting and dynamic to captivate them and interest them in the subject at hand. Strong evidence, a logical organizational structure, sound reasoning, and expert testimony will all help sway the audience to your way of thinking.

The Apathetic Audience

With this audience your job as a persuasive speaker becomes more difficult. An apathetic audience isn't necessarily opposed to you or your position, they just don't care about it. They see no connection between the topic and their lives. To be successful with this audience, you need to use many of the same techniques you would with a neutral audience. McCutcheon, Schaffer, and Wycoff also recommend a "dose of shock therapy" (364) with this type of audience. They tell how a teacher dealt with a group of low achieving students. They wouldn't listen to his advocacy of academics, because as they told him, all they wanted was to finish school so they could get jobs and buy items important to them, especially cars. The teacher used guest speakers to get through to these students. He brought in three business leaders from the community to explain what it would take to get hired and a car salesman to tell the students how much they would have to make to buy a car and pay for gas, insurance, and repairs. After hearing these speakers, the students vividly understood that they couldn't reach their goals unless they started valuing academics. They became far less apathetic.

The Opposed Audience

The opposed or hostile audience is against you and your opinions even before you begin speaking. Though this is the most difficult audience to face, there are steps you can take to give yourself a chance to reach them. Use a two-sided appeal (addressed later in this chapter) to show you understand how they feel. Demonstrate the qualities of goodwill and trustworthiness to show that, no matter what they think about you, you care about them. Try to find common ground and show that you are willing to compromise. Avoid needless confrontation.

Of course, you might face an audience that includes a mixture of all four types of listeners and you may, in that circumstance, need to combine approaches. Still, with most audiences, the majority of listeners will fall into one of these categories and you can significantly improve your chances of success if you modify your message to fit your audience.

Structuring a Persuasive Message

If you want to be effective at moving others to your way of thinking and feeling, you need to know more than how they are motivated and their predispositions. You also need to be able to structure and organize your arguments well. Especially for persuasive speakers, the organizational format can greatly influence the degree to which you influence others. Don't believe it? Let's say that two different people are interviewing for the same job. When asked the question, "What qualities do you have that would help you succeed in this job?" They answer as follows:

- **Candidate A:** I'm a real hard worker, so I'll do whatever you need me to. And I get to work on time and I never get sick. I like people, so I think I will get along with customers and my coworkers. Oh, yeah, I also have really good communication skills, too.

- **Candidate B:** I have three qualities that will help me excel in this job. First, I am a hard worker. I am willing to do any job and you'll never hear me complain or gripe. Second, I am punctual and reliable. You'll never have to worry about me coming late or calling in sick. Finally, I am good with people. I have strong communication skills and get along well with everyone.

Even though each of these candidates said essentially the same thing, it is much more likely that Candidate B would get the job. By structuring his response logically, he came across as more coherent and intelligent. Also, it is more likely that the interviewer will remember his answer. Thus, simply knowing different organizational formats can help you become better at influencing others.

Monroe's Motivated Sequence

Devised over sixty years ago by two university professors, Alan Monroe and Douglas Ehninger, Monroe's Motivated Sequence is one of the most popular and widely used formats for structuring a persuasive appeal (Gronbeck, et al. 243-47). Originally designed as a basis for sales presentations, the sequence has been used by millions of salespeople, students, and speakers since its inception. Monroe's Motivated Sequence is based on the principle of cognitive dissonance as speakers use it to alert listeners to a problem (creating dissonance) and then motivate them to seek a solution (resolving the dissonance). The sequence includes five steps:

attention, need, satisfaction, visualization, and action.

- **Attention.** First, you must wake up your audience and grab their attention. Make them want to listen to your speech. A surprising statement, a vivid illustration or story, a startling statistic, or a quotation can all accomplish this purpose. Franklin and Clark say, "Be accurate but bold. The goal is to make the audience a bit unsettled or anxious about the problem you are describing" (190).

- **Need.** Once you've captured the attention of the audience, show them why change is needed. Use evidence and strong reasoning to elicit concern. Facts, statistics, quotations, and case studies can all help you accomplish this purpose.

- **Satisfaction.** This is where you present your solution and demonstrate how your proposal will satisfy the need. Explain the elements of the solution and show how they will fix the problems you have described in the need step.

- **Visualization.** Here you ask the listeners to picture the future with or without your plan to intensify desire for your solution. This may be accomplished in one of three ways: by the positive method, the negative method, or the method of contrast. With the positive method, you describe how the future will look (and how much improved things will be) if your solution is implemented. In the negative method, you detail a world without your solution, depicting all the problems that will arise. Finally, with the method of contrast, you begin with the negative method and then move to the positive method to contrast the advantages of your plan to the disadvantages of not using it.

- **Action.** A persuasive message is useless unless you actually cause your listeners to do something. Two popular bumper stickers read "Visualize World Peace" and "Celebrate Diversity." While both have noble intentions, these appeals are useless. If I close my eyes and visualize world peace, we are no closer to that ideal than before. I could visualize myself with a million dollars, but it wouldn't help me make even one dollar! Therefore, in the action step, you tell the audience how they can play a role in helping the solution become a reality. Provide a few, clear, uncomplicated ideas as to what the audience can do.

I once heard a sales pitch for security supplies. The speaker began by attracting our attention by relating a personal story of how she was robbed and how vulnerable it made her feel. Next, she demonstrated need by stating a surplus of statistics and sharing a sampling of stories to illustrate how widespread crime really is. Her solution, of course, was for us to buy her wares. So, at the solution step, she showed us the plethora of products available for purchase, including pepper spray, a keychain with an alarm, and a fake home security system sign to scare off would-be robbers. She used positive visualization by telling stories of people who were fortunate enough to have her products available when they were confronted with danger and how they escaped unscathed. I am sure you can guess what her call to action was. She handed out order forms, urging us to buy as much as we could if we wanted to remain safe. Many people did spend a lot of money. Though this may not have been the most ethical use of Monroe's Motivated Sequence, it illustrates how it can be used with great success to move an audience to action.

Problem-Solution Order

Similar to the Motivated Sequence, but much simpler, the problem-solution format has only two parts. First, you demonstrate to your audience that a problem exists, then you propose a solution. For instance, you could show how much trash is generated in the world each day and that landfills are rapidly filling up. Then urge the audience to recycle. Or you could alert the audience to the problem of child abductions and then suggest they join the Neighborhood Watch.

Chronological Order

Also called time order, this method of organizing a persuasive appeal presents events or arguments in the order they happened.

For instance, you might focus on the past, present, and then the future in analyzing a problem. Or you may look at a problem across a number of years. Or you could outline a sequence of events leading up to a problem to provide a historical context and then present the solution as the possible next step in the process. Used primarily when a problem has a clear history, chronological organization can be effective because it follows a logical, familiar sequence. However, there is a danger that the listeners will become so wrapped up in the history of the problem that they miss the persuasive message.

Space Order

When using this organizational structure, a persuasive speaker organizes the message according to space or geography. For instance, when discussing violence in schools, a speaker might examine the problem in inner-city schools, suburban schools, and rural schools. If a speaker is addressing terrorism, he might look at terrorism abroad in one point and domestic terrorism in the next. Like chronological organization, space order is useful because it applies a structure that is already familiar to the audience.

Deductive Order

Deductive reasoning moves from general to specific. This is easy to remember because "deductive" sounds like "detective." A detective must start with a general fact (someone was murdered) and deduce specifics (how was the murder committed, who did it, what was the motive). Most essays written for high school and college classes use deductive organization. They begin with a general thesis and then use specific main points and examples to support the main idea.

Inductive Order

The opposite of deductive organization, inductive reasoning moves from specific facts to a general conclusion. For instance, at work you realize that the boss never calls you by name. Then you notice that other employees avoid you. You remember how people have left job postings on your desk and have asked if you need a reference for your resume. It finally dawns on you that you are going to be fired. You have used the evidence to reach a conclusion through inductive reasoning.

When using inductive order, you gradually lead your listeners to your thesis by helping them reason. You really just take them along with you so that it almost seems that they have reached the conclusion on their own. Consider the following line of reasoning:

- Crime has risen in our community in each of the last five years.

- Arrests have decreased in that amount of time.

- Our town has less police officers per capita than any other community in the state.

- A neighboring city, with roughly the same population, has twice as many police officers and significantly less crime than we have here.

After providing all these facts, and supporting them with evidence, the speaker would scarcely need to state the conclusion: our city needs to hire more police officers. The audience has probably figured it out on their own.

Cause and Effect

There is an old eighties song that says, "One thing leads to another." This is the premise of cause-effect reasoning. Cause-effect organization demonstrates that, when one event occurs, there will be an inevitable result. Therefore, if we want to avoid the consequence, we must avoid the cause. Or if we want the result, then we must strive to make the precipitating event happen. For instance, if you prove to an audience that heart disease is linked to a lack of exercise, you will be more successful in motivating them to start working out.

Comparison and Contrast

Using this format, a speaker discusses the pros and cons of two different plans, strategies, solutions, candidates, or ideas. Bouncing back and forth between the two options, you guide your audience to favor your perspective through direct comparison. You've probably seen an ad for a car that places the car being sold next to a competitor's model with two columns listing possible options and checkmarks to show which options each car has. Of course, the car being featured in the advertisement will have checks for each option while the other car will have only a few of the features. This is an example of comparison and contrast structure, and most likely a successful one. By examining such a direct comparison between vehicles, buyers feel as if they have really considered alternatives in their price range and chosen the one that offers the most for the money. Of course, this format can lead to card stacking. In the example of the car ad, the automaker will ignore options that the competitor's vehicle has that they don't provide on their car. Thus, you must always ask if all the pros and cons are being discussed when listening to a comparison and contrast message.

One-Sided vs. Two-Sided Messages

The comparison-contrast method of constructing a persuasive message brings up an important question: Is it better to present both sides of an argument or just the side you take? The answer? It depends. Research indicates there are times it is best to use each type of message.

When to Use a One-Sided Message

If the audience is inclined to be in agreement with your position, a one-sided message is best. This makes sense. If your listeners agree with you, why waste time trying to convince them that they are wrong? A candidate for public office, when speaking at a rally of his supporters, would not spend a considerable amount of time extolling the virtues of his opponent. However, if the audience is likely to be exposed to the other side at a later time, it may be best to use a two-sided message.

When to Use a Two-Sided Message

You will want to present both sides of an argument if the audience is initially opposed to your position. This will soften the audience to you and your stance because they will like and respect you for understanding where they are coming from. It is also a good idea because if the audience believes in the opposing side, they must be aware of arguments supporting that side. You also should present both sides of the issue when addressing an audience with higher levels of intelligence and educational attainment as they will be more likely to analyze your points and formulate opposing arguments while you speak.

If you do use a two-sided structure when making a persuasive appeal, it is essential that you refute the arguments opposing your viewpoint and demonstrate to the audience why the arguments supporting your position should be weighed more heavily. I've seen numerous students present arguments contradicting their own position in persuasive speeches, only to leave those arguments sitting untouched and not refuted at the end of the speech. If anything, these students convinced me to disagree with them! Now, suppose our candidate for office has left his supporters and is speaking to a group (let's say a teachers' union) that usually votes for candidates of the opposing party. He might say, "I know that most of you are planning to vote for my opponent and I'm sure it is because he has promised to raise taxes to help schools. While in office, he's only accomplished half of those goals. My opponent has repeatedly voted for tax increases, but has voted against three bills that would give money to schools. So, if you stick with him, you'll have less money in your school and in your pocket!" This is an effective use of a two-sided argument, because it shows the teachers that the candidate understands what's important to them and it creates dissonance in their minds through specific refutation of their beliefs.

Other Factors Influencing Persuasion

Because persuasion is such a complex process, there are numerous factors that influence us. We've already examined some of the major theories concerning persuasion, audience analysis, and the effects of organization on attitude change. According to research, the following elements also play a part in effecting persuasion:

Primacy and Recency

Studies have found (Bettinghaus and Cody, 147) that we best remember and are more influenced by what we hear first (a primacy effect) and last (a recency effect). The primacy effect is especially strong when the topic is of interest and familiar to the listeners, when the issues are seen as relatively unimportant, and when the presentation deals with a controversial subject. Studies done in the courtroom reveal that primacy effects are also strong when the receiver's goal is to make a decision about a person's character. The adage, "You never get a second chance to make a first impression," seems especially apt as we tend to make quick judgments about others and then cling tightly to those impressions. Recency effects are strongest when the subject being discussed is not interesting to the audience, when receivers are unfamiliar with the issues, and when the listeners are focusing on general topics and not the specific issue of a person's character.

Because of these findings, many speakers rightly place the most important information at the beginning and end of their presentation. If you are one of a group of presenters, such as in a series of job interviews or auditions, it might be to your benefit to present first or last. However, you can overcome the primacy and recency effects by making your message especially memorable and coherent. Other studies indicate that strong evidence is more important than any order effect in determining the success of a persuasive message.

Persuasive Language

One of the most successful persuasive messages in history is Martin Luther King, Jr.'s "I Have a Dream" speech. This speech is almost universally known, widely studied, and often quoted. Of course, there are many reasons that Dr. King's statement has had such impact. The importance of his message, the appropriateness of his ideas to the time period, and Dr. King's personal credibility all contribute to the impact of his speech. But perhaps more than any other factor, the language used by Dr. King makes the "I Have a Dream" speech so powerful and memorable. If you want to be more persuasive, whether you are addressing an individual or a group, whether you are communicating in person or in writing, you must use persuasive language. Strive for the following:

- **Imagery.** Use colorful adjectives and adverbs to create vivid descriptions that will linger in the minds of your listeners. One speaker, in order to make a quotation by Michelangelo more memorable, described in poetic language his painting on the ceiling of the Sistine Chapel. "Reds as true as blood," she said, "flow through the chapel in concert with tender teals. Gentle greens and vibrant violets dance upon the vaulted ceiling."

- **Analogies.** Comparisons between two things that at first glance seem unrelated help your listeners better understand your argument. A speaker who extolled the virtues of American capitalism compared the American economic system to a symphony. "Individual instruments, when all played together, make beautiful music. Likewise, individual entrepreneurs, all working together, create a symphony of economic success."

- **Poetic Elements.** Rhyme, alliteration, assonance, and parallelism can all add impact to a persuasive appeal. Martin Luther King's speech owes much of its success to the parallelism Dr. King used by repeating "I Have a Dream" throughout his message. In his inaugural address, President George W. Bush used alliteration when he said, "Today we affirm a new commitment to live out our nation's promise through civility, courage, compassion, and character."

- **Vivid Illustration.** One of the most successful series of books ever to be published is the *Chicken Soup for the Soul* texts. If you are one of the five people who haven't seen any of these books, they are a collection of motivational and inspirational stories on a variety of topics. I believe that these books owe their success to the stories they feature. Rather than lecturing readers, they inspire through examples and vivid illustration. You can use this technique, too. Sprinkle your appeals with stories about yourself, people you know, and famous individuals. Doing so will make your presentation more interesting, memorable, and persuasive.

Fear

Driver's education teachers show films of terrible accidents that resulted from unsafe driving. Public Service Announcements tell us that one in three smokers die as a result of their habit. These are examples of fear appeals, which are designed to frighten an individual into a certain way of thinking or behaving. Do they work? A classic study by Janis and Feshbach examined the effects of fear appeals on dental hygiene (Bettinghaus and Cody, 159). The subjects, all students at the same high school, attended three different lectures on tooth decay. The different lectures used mild, moderate, and strong fear appeals. As you might expect, the results showed that fear appeals do work. What you might not expect, however, is that the students who were exposed to mild fear appeals showed the most improvement in their dental hygiene habits.

In addition to proving the effectiveness of fear appeals, this and other studies also demonstrate that the strength of the fear appeal must be related to the change desired. The simple act of brushing your teeth may not have seemed like a feasible way to prevent the horrible disfigurement used to scare students in the strong fear appeal group, rendering that lecture less effective than the one that more realistically presented the problems resulting from not brushing.

Another factor influencing the effectiveness of fear appeals is the relevance of the threat to the listener. People are only affected if they believe it could actually happen to them. Another study found that fear appeals designed to get people to build a fallout shelter were more effective with younger people who had children (Bettinghaus and Cody, 159). People without children have less responsibility and, therefore, less concern for their own safety. This is why so many of those fear appeals used in driver's education classes don't work. Adolescents too often feel invincible and believe they could not be involved in such an accident. It often takes the death of a friend or a classmate for young drivers to become more careful.

Finally, fear appeals are best when the action being suggested is likely to work. Someone may feel that the flu is undesirable and that they are susceptible to it, but have doubts concerning the effectiveness of flu shots. No matter how many fear appeals this individual encounters encouraging him to get a shot, he will probably not do so.

So to use fear appeals effectively, you must make the threat seem harmful but not exaggerated, real to your listeners, and the solution you suggest must seem like it would work. A more important question is whether you should use fear appeals. Obviously, ethics dictates that you not use them in a tricky or manipulative way. You must truly believe that your audience will face serious consequences if they don't follow your advice. Otherwise, they will see through your sophistry and your credibility will suffer.

Groups

According to Erwin P. Bettinghaus and Michael J. Cody, "The political analyst and the opinion polling expert base their predictions on a single assumption: *People who are alike tend to vote alike*" (62). They also tend to think alike, act alike, and buy alike. This is why politicians cater to "the female vote" or "the elderly vote," and advertisers target market demographics. We are influenced by the following types of groups:

- **Reference groups** are any group that we use to compare our attitudes, beliefs, or abilities. For instance, in order for a young athlete to consider himself a good baseball player, he needs a basis of comparison. He will most likely use the other players on his Little League team as his reference point. A teenager might choose her clothes or hairstyle based on the opinions of the "popular" kids at her school.

- **Demographic groups** are determined by characteristics such as age, gender, and race. These are involuntary membership groups to which we belong because of reasons that are beyond our control. For this reason, demographic groups tend to be a less reliable measure of an individual's attitudes than other groups.

- **Voluntary groups**, including professional and service organizations, fraternities and sororities, churches, political parties, recreational athletic leagues, and study groups, are organizations that we willingly join.

It can be dangerous to assume that individuals share attitudes, opinions, and beliefs simply because they belong to the same group. Further, all of us belong to a number of groups simultaneously. Still, you can use groups to increase your effectiveness in persuasive situations by mentioning reference groups to your listeners and using them to analyze your audience. As a receiver, you must also be aware of the power of groups. Ask yourself if you truly believe the message when you encounter persuasion or if you are simply going along with a group to which you belong.

Nonverbals

As you already learned in Chapter Four, nonverbal communication can be very powerful. This is no less true in the area of persuasion. Generally, speakers have been found to be more persuasive when they maintain eye contact, stand closer to their listeners (but not too close), use more illustrative gestures, have less disfluencies and fillers, speak at a moderately quick rate, and avoid throaty, tense, and nasal tones.

Humor

What are the best commercials you've ever seen? List a few that stand out from the thousands of advertisements you've seen in your life. Chances are, the ads you thought of are humorous. Though humor alone cannot affect persuasion, it can certainly make a persuasive message more effective. It helps gain and maintain the attention of the audience, makes the message more memorable, builds rapport between the speaker and the audience, and makes the listeners less resistant to persuasion.

Conclusion

Glenn Van Ekeren (291) tells the story of a traveling evangelist who returned home from a revival. When his wife asked what he spoke on, he replied, "Charity. I told the audience it was the privilege and responsibility of the rich to give to the poor."

"How did they respond?" she asked.

"So-so," replied the evangelist. "I convinced the poor."

Persuading others to your way of thinking is, at best, difficult. Like the traveling evangelist, you will never succeed in convincing everyone that you are right. Still, there will be numerous times when you find it necessary to attempt to persuade others. There will be even more occasions when you are confronted with persuasive messages. So, to be a competent communicator, you must understand how attitudes, opinions, and actions are influenced.

Chapter Seven

Leadership Skills

Lessons from Geese

In 1993, Robert Fulghum wrote a very popular book titled, *All I Really Need to Know I Learned in Kindergarten*. The thesis of the essay from which the book took its title is that all the really important lessons in life — share, play fair, take a nap every afternoon — are taught in kindergarten. To paraphrase Robert Fulghum, all we really need to know about leading and following can be taught by geese. Based on the work of Milton Olson and transcribed from a speech given by Angeles Arrien at the 1991 Organizational Development Network, "Lessons From Geese" proves that we can learn much from our flying friends.

Fact: As each goose flaps its wings, it creates an uplift for the birds that follow. By flying in a "V" formation, each bird gains a 71 percent greater flying range.

Lesson: People who share a common goal can get where they are going more quickly and easily when they rely on each other's support and strength.

Fact: When a goose falls out of formation, it suddenly feels the drag and resistance of flying alone. It quickly moves back into formation to take advantage of the lifting power of the bird in front of it.

Lesson: If we had as much sense as a goose, we would work with others who are headed where we want to go. Getting there will be easier if we are willing to accept their help and give our help in return.

Fact: When the lead goose tires, it moves back into the formation and allows another goose to fly to the point position.

Lesson: It pays to share leadership. People who are

interdependent and recognize each other's skills, strengths, and unique gifts a have greater opportunity of reaching their goals.

Fact: The geese flying in formation honk to encourage those up front to keep up their speed.

Lesson: Productivity is much greater in groups where there is encouragement. Leaders need to be encouraged by their followers and followers need the encouragement of their leaders.

Fact: When a goose gets sick or wounded, two geese drop out of formation and follow it down to help and protect it. They stay with it until it dies or is able to fly again. Then they launch out with another formation or catch up with their original flock.

Lesson: If we have as much sense as geese, we will stand by each other in difficult times as well as when we are strong.

As this illustration shows, groups need both leaders and followers to be successful. There will be times when you are expected to take charge and other times when you must follow the lead of someone else. Therefore, this chapter will help you understand what it means to lead and show you how to develop the skills necessary to become an effective leader as well as discussing what it takes to be an effective team member.

The Value of Leading

Leadership is a valuable and much sought after skill. No matter who you are or what you do, you probably hope to gain enough respect and esteem that you will be considered a leader. If you are a professional, you hope to be placed in charge of projects and receive promotions. If you are an athlete, you want to be the player to whom your teammates look for direction. If you are a teacher, you strive to earn the respect and admiration of your students. Harold Green is considered a leader in the world of business, having built ITT from a small company into a huge conglomerate. He says, "Leadership is the very heart and soul of business management ... What you manage in business is people ... To my mind, the quality of leadership is the single most important ingredient in the recipe of business success" (Van Ekeren, 225).

What Is Leadership?

President Dwight D. Eisenhower gave perhaps the best definition of leadership. He said, "Leadership is the art of getting someone else to do something you want done because he wants to do it." Leaders are people who, through their competence, charisma, vision, and integrity, make others want to follow. McCutcheon, Schaffer, and Wycoff identify two components of leadership. Leaders, they say, effectively motivate themselves as well as uniting others to work together to accomplish a certain task (642). They also note that leadership is the culmination of other communication skills, as a leader must be a good listener, able to work well within a group, organized, able to use logic and reasoning, and able to persuade others. Thus, by discussing many of those skills, the preceding chapters in this book have already begun to prepare you to become a leader.

How Do You Become a Leader?

In his play *Twelfth Night*, William Shakespeare wrote, "Some are born great, some achieve greatness, and some have greatness thrust upon them." Shakespeare realized that people become leaders in different ways. In fact, there are three ways to attain a position of leadership:

Appointed Leaders

If a person or a group of people with the power to do so select you to a position of authority, you are an appointed leader. A business manager is hired or promoted by the CEO or owner of the business; the leader of a class discussion group may be selected by the teacher; the principal of a school is chosen by a hiring committee. All of these individuals are appointed leaders.

Elected Leaders

Elected leaders are chosen though a vote. The President of the United States, a union representative, the chair of the local school board, and the members of the student government at a high school or college are all elected to their positions of leadership.

Emerged Leaders

Some leaders, rather than being formally chosen by an individual or a group, emerge naturally. Because of their ability and personality, others look to these individuals for guidance whether or not they have a formal title or any real authority. In sports, players may say that one of their teammates has become a "team leader." In business, the people who do the finest work tend to garner more respect than their peers. In a classroom, the best student is often asked for help or expected to take charge on group projects.

Types of Leaders

There are three basic styles of leadership: democratic, authoritarian, and laissez faire. No one style of leadership is inherently superior to the others; rather, each has its place depending on the situation and the task at hand.

Democratic Leaders

A democratic leader provides direction but allows followers to determine the best way to achieve goals. A democratic leader solicits input from group members, shares power, seeks consensus, and motivates group members to seek self-direction and self-actualization. In most situations, democratic leaders are the most popular because followers feel valued and the input given by group members provides the leader with more information, which leads to better decisions. The democratic style of leadership is most appropriate when there is plenty of time available to make decisions and when all members have approximately the same level of knowledge or expertise.

Authoritarian Leaders

If one person is completely in charge of the group and makes all the decisions without consulting the members of the group, he or she is an authoritarian leader. This style of leadership is best when there is an emergency and it is necessary for the person with the most knowledge and expertise to take control. For this reason, the military uses an authoritarian style of leadership. In battle, soldiers must take orders from their commander. Can you imagine an army that votes on the best way to attack the enemy? They would be overrun before they even began to fight!

Authoritarian leadership is also appropriate when group members remain unmotivated and unfocused despite efforts to accomplish goals in a democratic manner. For instance, a teacher may experiment with lessons that require students to take control of their learning by designing their own projects and setting their own deadlines. If the students are unable to do this and end up wasting most of their time, the teacher will have to step in and run the class in a less democratic manner.

Finally, the authoritarian style is most suitable when the leader has far more experience and knowledge than the followers. Imagine that a group of high school students volunteer to help a carpenter build a ramp to help a handicapped individual get into his home. It wouldn't make sense for the carpenter to seek input from the students, who most likely have no training or experience in carpentry. Rather, he would tell them exactly what needs to be done and how to do it.

Laissez Faire Leaders

Usually used to describe the economic philosophy of limited government intervention, the term laissez faire literally means "to let people do as they choose." Thus, laissez faire leaders adopt a hands-off style by providing minimal direction and authority. They answer questions, but only when a group member actively seeks out the leader's advice. This type of leadership is usually the least effective for accomplishing group goals, because the group has no focus or direction and the leader is seen as completely nonthreatening. The only time the laissez faire style is preferred is in social situations. At a party, the host might make some minimal preparations but then leave the guests alone to enjoy themselves unless asked for something specifically by one of the guests such as a drink refill or directions to the restroom.

The best leader is one who knows how and when to apply each style of leadership. A high school principal, for instance, would be expected to demonstrate the authoritarian style of leadership during a fire drill, the democratic style at a teacher's meeting, and the laissez faire style while chaperoning a school dance. Too often, unfortunately, leaders try to use the same leadership style across all situations. This causes frustration among the group members and makes the group less effective.

The Qualities of Effective Leaders

While one attribute of effective leadership is adapting to specific situations, there are many qualities that strong leaders must always exhibit. If you hope to be a respected leader whom others willingly follow, you must strive to demonstrate the following:

Effective Leaders Have Vision

As a leader, you must know what you want, why you want it, and how you plan to get it. Followers want to know the greater purpose toward which they are working. When the framers of the Constitution of the United States drafted the document that would govern their country, they envisioned a nation that would provide liberty and freedom to all its citizens. In the preamble of the Constitution, they indicated that their purpose was to "form a more perfect Union, establish Justice, insure domestic Tranquility, provide for the common Defense, promote the general Welfare, and secure the Blessings of Liberty to ourselves and our Posterity." This vision has been shared by millions of Americans who have struggled and even given their lives to uphold those principles through the years (by striving to end slavery, seeking suffrage for the disenfranchised, and fighting to end tyranny abroad). The greatness of America can be explained, in part, by the fact that the founding fathers had a vision of what they hoped their country would become.

The most successful business leaders also demonstrate vision. In 1978, childhood friends Ben Cohen and Jerry Greenfield opened an ice cream shop in a renovated gas station in Burlington, Vermont. Since then, Ben and Jerry's Homemade Ice Cream has expanded into one of the largest and best-known brands in the world. Much of Ben and Jerry's success comes from the way they view business. As their business began to grow, the partners wrote a Statement of Mission, which, according to their website (www.benjerry.com), is "a new corporate concept of linked prosperity" and has three parts. Ben and Jerry strive to create the finest product possible, create a sound financial basis, and improve the quality of life locally, nationally, and globally. Ben and Jerry have been successful in accomplishing all three goals. They actively work on numerous social causes (Ben Cohen has even written a book on how to run a values-led business), have remained profitable, and if you've ever tasted their ice cream, you know they produce a darn good product! It is this vision that has, to a large degree, set Ben and Jerry apart from the millions of other people who have enjoyed far less success in the ice cream business.

Effective Leaders Are Willing to Act

It is not enough to simply have a vision. You must also work to make that vision a reality. Nolan Bushell, the founder of Atari, describes the secret of his success. "The critical ingredient is getting off your butt and doing something. It's as simple as that," Bushell asserts. "A lot of people have ideas, but there are few who decide to do something about them" (Van Ekeren, 16-17).

There is an old joke about a man who is so poor he prays to God to allow him to win the lottery. He continues to ask God every night for a year that he would have the winning ticket. Finally, he becomes frustrated, falls to his knees, and prays, "I've prayed every night for a year to win the lottery, yet you have ignored my pleas." Suddenly a big voice booms from the sky, "I've heard your prayers, but give me a break. The least you could do is buy a lottery ticket!"

Effective Leaders Treat Different People Differently

Not everyone learns the same way or is motivated in the same way. Effective leaders realize this and treat their followers differently. Of course, you must not deal with your followers in an unfair or unjust manner or show favoritism, but you should use different techniques to explain something to an auditory learner than you would a kinesthetic learner. You should know who is best motivated by deadlines and who works well without time pressures. You should know how much tact to use when criticizing different group members. To do so, you must communicate openly with your followers and get to know each of them well.

Effective Leaders Make Good Decisions

If you are a leader, there will come a time when you must make decisions that will affect not only you, but all of your followers. If you are a strong leader, you will make good decisions. Imagine you are a football coach. It's fourth down and goal with the ball on the opponent's one-yard line. Your team trails by five points, so you need a touchdown to win. There is time for only one more play. What do you call? Should you hand the ball off to the fullback up the middle or have the quarterback throw a pass? How about a trick play to surprise the defense? The entire game, and the fan's estimation of your leadership ability, rests on this one decision.

To make good decisions, you must be prepared, knowledgeable about the issues and the people involved, able to prioritize, and aware of the risks. In our example, you will be more equipped to call the right play if you know the abilities of your players, as well as the tendencies and weaknesses of the defense. You know that the other team likes to stack their defense on the line of scrimmage in goal-line situations, so you have the quarterback fake a handoff, drawing the defense to the running back, and then throw a pass to a wide open receiver. Your preparation and knowledge have enabled you to make the right decision.

Effective Leaders Take Risks

No matter how prepared you are, you will sometimes make the wrong decision. Does that ruin your ability to lead? Of course not! In fact, another characteristic of effective leaders is that they take risks and are not afraid to fail. Robert Schuller says, "The people who are really failures are the people who set their standards so low, keep the bar at such a safe level, that they never run the risk of failure" (Van Ekeren, 153).

Henry Ford went broke five times before he found success. Abraham Lincoln lost five elections before he finally became President. Charles Darrow's idea for a board game was initially rejected by Parker Brothers, who cited "52 fundamental errors" with the game. Eventually, Parker Brothers changed their minds and Monopoly went on to become the most popular board game ever.

Thomas Edison tried over ten thousand different experiments before he finally demonstrated the first incandescent light bulb on October 21, 1879. When asked if he was frustrated by his failures, Edison replied, "I have not failed. I've just found 10,000 ways that won't work." As long as your failure comes from a desire to do something great and not incompetence, your followers will not desert you because you make mistakes.

An Effective Leader Handles Conflict Well

As you learned in Chapter Five, conflict is inevitable. However, when you are a leader, your followers look to you to help them manage and resolve problems. First, you can help your followers avoid conflict with you and with each other by treating them fairly and creating a harmonious environment. When conflicts do occur, you must use the principles of conflict management to turn potentially negative situations into positives.

An Effective Leader Makes Sacrifices

If you think that being a leader entitles you to special treatment or perks, you will not be effective in your leadership position. In his book *Leadership Is an Art*, Max De Pree says, "The first responsibility of a leader is to define reality. The last is to say thank you. In between, the leader is a servant." Alexander the Great, Macedonian conqueror of Asia, slept on the ground with his troops, refused to eat if there was no food for his men, and led his army into every battle. He realized his followers would not respect him if he put himself above them and asked for preferential treatment. Mother Teresa is known as one of the greatest religious leaders of all time, yet she lived in poverty and spent her life caring for others.

Leading a Group Meeting

One of the primary responsibilities of a leader is to run group meetings. If you are called on to do so, you are expected to accomplish the following:

Make All Necessary Preparations

As a leader, you must arrange for a place for the group to meet, prepare all necessary supplies and materials, inform members of the purpose of the meeting, and make sure all group members are familiar with each other.

Begin the Meeting

It is your job to ensure that the meeting starts on time, make introductions and announcements, and establish the agenda, or schedule, of the meeting. Be sure all group members know why they are meeting and what you hope to accomplish.

Stimulate Discussion

You must solicit input from group members and make sure everyone contributes to discussion. If group interaction begins to stall, you must prod the group through pointed questions.

Identify and Counteract Major Group Problems

If a member hogs the conversation, becomes overly argumentative, or attempts to distract the group members from their purpose by constantly cracking jokes or complaining, it is up to you to speak to that individual and to stop such behavior. If the group gets off track, refocus them on the issue at hand. Be aware of conflicts and work to resolve them constructively.

End the Meeting

Before you adjourn, summarize the meeting to review what the group accomplished, establish a time for the next meeting, and be sure members know what is expected of them before you see them again.

Preparing Yourself to Lead

We've seen that leadership is a valuable skill, but a difficult thing to do well. So how can you prepare yourself to lead capably when the opportunity arises? In the book *Leadership: A Communication Perspective*, Michael Z. Hackman and Craig E. Johnson identify three components of leadership development (211-14):

Leadership Learning

Reading this chapter is a first step, but you should not stop there. The more you know about theories of leadership, the better prepared you'll be to lead. Also, you can study other leaders to help you develop your own leadership style. Hackman and Johnson say, "We can learn a great deal from the experiences of other leaders. We will want to adopt some of their strategies and behaviors; others we will want to avoid" (211).

Leadership Experience

Volunteer for any activity that can provide leadership experience at school, church, work, or in the community. If you are a student, run for student government or volunteer to coordinate a campus activity. At work, strive to become a manager or a crew leader. When the experience is over, reflect on it. What did you do well? What more could you have done? How will you lead differently next time you have an opportunity to do so?

Find a Mentor

Especially in the workplace, you can increase your chances of emerging as a leader if you find someone to mentor you. The term "mentor" is taken from Homer's *Odyssey*. The character Mentor, friend of the ancient Greek King Ulysses, watched the king's son while Ulysses was away, acting as a counselor and guide to the young man. A mentor can help you learn the ropes, serve as a role model, give friendship and counseling, and provide sponsorship by fighting for your proposals and mentioning your name for promotions. Hackman and Johnson cite a survey of all the executives who appeared in the "Who's News" column of the *Wall Street Journal*. Two-thirds reported having one or more mentors during their careers and most stated that their sponsors had either an "extraordinary or substantial influence" on their careers (214).

Being an Effective Team Member

For groups to function effectively, there must be both leaders and followers. Classrooms have teachers and students. Workplaces have bosses and employees. Theatrical productions have directors and actors. As vital as leadership skills are, you will not be the leader of every group to which you belong. It therefore becomes very important for you to learn the skills of following.

127

Problem Team Members

I'm sure you've encountered them. They get in the way, cause discussion to get off track, and create difficulties in the group. Franklin and Clark (137-38) identify the following types of group members that prevent groups from operating as effectively as they should:

- **Whiners.** When asked to do something, whiners complain and make excuses instead of pulling their weight.

- **Glory hogs.** Rather than helping the team accomplish their goals, glory hogs want to take credit for the group's successes. They talk too much, interrupt, and always want to be in the spotlight.

- **Grouches.** Especially frustrating team members, grouches argue for the sake of argument, disagree with everyone, and find fault with every proposal. Grouches are a drain on groups, sapping energy from other team members.

- **Bullies.** And you thought you were through with bullies when you left elementary school! Bullies criticize, intimidate, blame, and ridicule others in group meetings.

- **Clams.** Like the animals they are named after, clams bury themselves in the sand. They spend their time acting bored, daydreaming, and doodling. Consequently, they add nothing to group interaction.

- **Clowns.** Injecting a little humor into group interaction is a good thing. Clowns, however, take it too far. They constantly goof around, distracting the other members of the group.

- **Sidetrackers.** By bringing up irrelevant topics, sidetrackers get the group off the issue at hand, which makes it impossible for the other group members to accomplish their goals.

If you find yourself filling one of these roles in any group to which you belong, knock it off! You will only make everyone else angry and ensure that the group cannot get anything done. A better tactic is to ask yourself why you are behaving as you are and then deal with the root cause of your frustration constructively. For instance, you may be playing the grouch at work, picking fights with your coworkers and finding fault with all of their work. If you think about it, you might realize that your mood is a result of troubles at home. By dealing with those troubles, you will be more productive at work.

Being a Good Team Member

So the first step in being an effective team member is to avoid behavior that causes problems. But you also want to make a positive contribution to whatever group you belong. How can you fulfill your role as an employee, student, group member, or follower to the best of your ability? Here are some suggestions to assist you in helping your organization:

- **Participate.** You are of no use to any group if you are unwilling to speak, offer ideas, advocate for your perspective, or work.

- **Be group oriented.** Actually, this applies whether you are a leader or a follower. Employees who are more concerned with getting a promotion than helping the company make money are of no use to their employers. Athletes who would rather build their own statistics than fulfill a specific role that helps the team win only get in the way. When you are a part of a group, you should put aside your selfish interests and use your talents, abilities, knowledge, and insights to help the group achieve its goals and objectives.

- **Do your job.** If you promise or are asked to do something, follow through. Complete every task you undertake to the best of your ability.

- **Take the initiative.** As a speech and debate coach, I have had the privilege of working with many outstanding students. However, two stand out because they not only did what was asked of them, they also saw things that could be done to help the team and did them on their own. Brian Cleveland started a team newsletter that he wrote every month and created a phone tree to spread news quickly. Micah Hardt constructed a box of games to pass the time at tournaments, designed and purchased T-shirts for the team, and tabulated an entire tournament that our school hosted. These students not only had good ideas, they also saw those ideas through to completion.

- **Be open-minded.** When others make proposals, listen to them with an open mind. If everyone comes to the group with their minds already made up, group members will argue for their own positions rather than striving for compromise or looking for unique solutions to problems.

- **But be critical.** Being open-minded doesn't mean you should blindly accept the proposals of others. Listen carefully when others speak and analyze their ideas critically. One of the benefits of working in a group is that the pooling of talent, ideas, and knowledge yields greater results than any one group member could provide on his or her own. Thus, you can help others by critiquing, modifying, and refining their ideas.

- **Center conflict on issues, not personalities.** When you disagree with others, make it clear that you are opposed to their ideas, not to them. Never engage in personal attacks, name calling, or insults. Likewise, if someone else opposes your suggestions, don't take it personally. Consider their criticism carefully. Who knows? They may be able to improve upon your ideas.

- **Ensure understanding.** When you speak, be clear and concise. Ask for feedback to make sure others understand what you have said. Help clarify if you perceive that other group members don't understand what someone has said. It is also a good idea to begin your statements with paraphrases. For instance, you might respond to another employee's suggestion at work by saying, "As I understand, you believe that employees with seniority should get to choose their hours first. Is that right? I understand why you feel that way, but I don't think it's a practical solution. Let me tell you why … "

- **Encourage others.** Congratulate others on a job well done. Commend good ideas. Urge others to speak. Give credit where credit is due. Even in difficult times, try to keep a positive attitude to keep yourself and the rest of the group energized.

Effective Following Is a Form of Leadership

The irony is that if you use these suggestions for being an effective follower, you may very well make yourself so valuable to the organization that you become a leader. This could happen in two ways. First, you may become either an appointed or an elected leader as others recognize your proficiency and select you when a position of authority becomes available. If you are an outstanding employee, you may be promoted to management. If you are an active member of a school club, you might be elected to a position of authority in that group. Still, even if there is no formal position of leadership available, your competence may cause others to regard you as an emerged leader in the group. So there is a fine line between effective leaders and followers. Both are committed to others, both put group goals ahead of their own self-interests, and both serve others.

A Leader

I went on a search to become a leader.

I searched high and low. I spoke with authority. People listened. But, alas, there was one who was wiser than I, and they followed that individual.

I sought to inspire confidence, but the crowd responded, "Why should we trust you?"

I postured, and I assumed the look of leadership with a countenance that flowed with confidence and pride. But many passed me by and never noticed my air of elegance.

I ran ahead of the others, pointing the way to new heights. I demonstrated that I knew the route to greatness. And then I looked back, and I was alone.

131

"What shall I do?" I queried. "I've tried hard and used all that I know. And I sat down and pondered long.

And then I listened to the voices around me. And I heard what the group was trying to accomplish. I rolled up my sleeves and joined in the work.

As we worked, I asked, "Are we all together in what we want to do and how to get the job done?"

And we thought together, and we fought together, and we struggled towards our goal.

I found myself encouraging the fainthearted. I sought the ideas of those too shy to speak out. I taught those who had little skill. I praised those who worked hard. When our task was completed, one of the group turned to me and said, "This would not have been done but for your leadership."

At first, I said, "I didn't lead. I just worked hard with the rest." And then I understood, leadership is not a goal. It's a way of reaching a goal.

I lead best when I help others to go where we've decided to go. I lead best when I help others to use themselves creatively. I lead best when I forget about myself as a leader and focus on my group, their needs and their goals.

To lead is to serve. To give. To achieve together.

Anonymous

Conclusion

Now that you know what is expected of leaders and followers as well as the characteristics of each, you have the basic tools to fulfill both roles as competently as possible. Doing so will improve your life, both personally and professionally, in innumerable ways.

Chapter Eight

Family Communication

An old Chinese proverb states, "A family in harmony will prosper in everything." Certainly this is as true today as ever. Your family should be a refuge, a safe harbor for you after a tumultuous day on the seas of life. Healthy families provide love, support, security, safety, and self-esteem. As a part of a family structure, children learn who they are, as individuals and as members of a larger group. Most likely, you will have no relationship more intimate or meaningful than you have with the members of your family.

However, the sad fact is that families are not always "in harmony." Families frequently struggle with conflict and don't know how to communicate with each other. Too often, these problems contribute to the end of marriages. In America, more than half of first marriages end in divorce. According to Reuters News Service, the ramifications of such problems are immense. After a two-year study, the authors of *Marriage in America: A Report to the Nation*, concluded that the decline of marriage is mainly responsible for the deteriorating well-being of children. The authors, Sociology Professor David Popenoe of Rutgers University and Jean Bethke Elshtain, Professor of Social and Political Ethics at the University of Chicago Divinity School, assert, "If we're concerned about teen pregnancies, illegitimacy, deadbeat dads, and children in poverty, then we can no longer ignore the common denominator behind these problems — the steady weakening of marriage as the primary institution for raising children."

Even when families don't break up, the inability to communicate effectively is harmful to all members of the family. Unhealthy communication patterns, covert manipulation, and a lack of discipline can irreparably damage relationships between spouses, siblings, and parents and children. Therefore, this chapter

133

will help you recognize and eliminate such destructive communication patterns while using productive strategies to keep your family relationships healthy and harmonious.

What Is a Family — And What Is Family Communication?

The study of family structures has become much more broad over the years. The idea of a "traditional nuclear family," with a mother, father, and one or more children, has become outmoded. In the real world, there are single-parent families, blended and mixed families, foster families, and an increasing number of grandparents raising their grandchildren. Therefore, we will define family broadly as a group of related people who share common living space. As Raymond Zeuschner points out, a family may be related "by commitment, economic need, living quarters, interdependence, biology, marriage, or a combination of these factors" (350). Family communication is the interaction that develops among those people over time.

The element of time in family communication is significant, because unlike so many other instances of interpersonal communication, we live and interact with the members of our family over the course of many years. This magnifies unhealthy communication patterns and increases the stakes of communication. While you can flee conflicts with neighbors, a rude customer, your auto mechanic, and classmates, you are stuck with your family. This makes it even more imperative that you learn healthy ways of communicating with your loved ones.

Types of Family Relationships

A series of studies done both in the United States and internationally have determined that marriages can be subdivided into three basic types: traditionals, separates, and independents (DeVito, 267).

Traditionals
Traditional couples see themselves more in terms of the family

than as separate individuals. They share the same belief system and basic life philosophy, spend a lot of time together, and place a great deal of importance on home and family life. Because spouses adhere to traditional gender roles, there are rarely any role conflicts. Due to the emphasis traditionals place on marriage and family, they usually don't consider separation or divorce.

Independents

While independents value family, they believe that maintaining individual identities is more important. They have a strong sense of self and spend a great deal of time together, but also have outside friends and interests.

Separates

Though separates live together, their relationship is more like that of roommates than family. They have little desire to be together and rarely are, except at ritual functions such as family meals, holidays, and outside social activities. Each person in this type of relationship has their own space, interests, and schedule. Often, marriages of this type are more the result of convenience or the meeting of societal norms than of love and interdependence.

Couples may also be a combination of these types. For instance, if one spouse is a traditional and the other an independent, their relationship would be a traditional/independent split. Understanding what type of family you have is primary to understanding your relationships and communication patterns.

Communication Patterns within Families

Another way to classify families is through the way they communicate with each other. Rather than looking at the attitudes of couples and families, the following classifications are the result of how spouses and members of the family actually interact.

The Equality Pattern

In this type of relationship, there is no leader or follower as each person shares equally in discussion and decision-making. Conflicts are not viewed as harmful by the members of the family, but rather as an opportunity to exchange ideas and find mutually beneficial resolutions. Couples that use this communication pattern rarely engage in power struggles as their arguments usually center on conflict and not on relational issues.

The Balanced Split Pattern

This relationship also has equality among the participants, but each person has authority over different aspects of family life. In a traditional family that uses this pattern, the husband may be the breadwinner and in charge of issues such as home repair and automobile maintenance. The wife may be more responsible for child care and housework. Other families may divide these areas differently.

The Unbalanced Split Pattern

As in the balanced split pattern, authority is divided among individuals in this pattern of family communication, but in an unequal way. One person has control over more than half the areas of authority, and therefore over the relationship as well. The person in control makes the important decisions, dictates to the others what will be done, and states his or her opinion more frequently.

The Monopoly Pattern

In this type of family, one person is the controlling authority. That individual does not ask questions or seek the advice of other family members, but rather lectures and makes demands of them. Conflict is rare in families that use this pattern because everyone knows who has the power and who will win. The noncontrolling individuals look to the person in control for permission and for decision-making.

Usually, these patterns arise depending on the needs and personal characteristics of the individuals involved. For instance, in a marriage between a person with a high need to be led and an individual with a controlling nature, the unbalanced split or monopoly patterns may actually work best. Therefore, it is difficult to assert that any one pattern is inherently better than the others no matter how unhealthy the latter two may seem at first glance.

Birth Order Effects

In recent years, a great deal of research has been done on how the order in which children are born into their family influences their personality. While it is always dangerous to make broad generalizations about such a complex thing as human behavior, birth order is an interesting field of study that can provide insight into yourself and others. Lorie M. Sutter of Ohio State University asserts, "Birth order research may offer 'clues' about why people tend to be the way they are. Through your (birth order) you develop your behavior pattern, way of thinking, and emotional response. Your birth order helps determine your expectations, your strategies for dealing with people and your weaknesses." As you read through the characteristics of first-born, middle-born, and last-born children, see if they fit you and those you know.

First-Born and Only Children

First-borns are typically highly motivated to achieve. They are responsible, goal-setters, organized, and often perfectionists. In school, they work harder and get better grades than children born later. Sutter points out that "any enumeration of prominent people, eminent scholars, even presidents of the United States contains a high percent of first-borns." Approximately 90 percent of the astronauts who have been sent into outer space have been first-borns.

Middle-Born Children

Middle children never have their parents to themselves. As a result, they become good at negotiation and compromise and tend to be more flexible, generous, and diplomatic. Interestingly, they are also more competitive (probably because they are always fighting for attention). Because of these traits, they make excellent managers and leaders.

Last-Born Children

Youngest children tend to have good people skills. They are more outgoing and great at motivating others. Last-borns also tend to be affectionate, uncomplicated, creative, willing to take risks, and sometimes a little absent-minded. Consequently, last-born children make good salespeople.

Family Communication Disorders

We've already discussed how devastating it can be when families don't communicate in a healthy way. According to McKay, Davis, and Fanning, this happens when family members "are prohibited from expressing certain feelings, needs, or awarenesses" (219). There are four primary family communication disorders that restrict openness and direct communication. Knowing these disorders is the first step to overcoming them.

Denial

Rather than directly expressing needs and engaging in healthy conflict, some families deny that any problem exists. Denial can be either overt, which involves statements like, "I'm fine," and "I don't want anything," or covert, which can involve withdrawing physically or emotionally.

Deletion

A form of passive communication, deletion occurs when family members make statements but omit one important part: their wants and needs. For instance, a wife might say, "We have nothing in the refrigerator," when she really means, "I'd rather not cook tonight. Can we go out to eat?" A father may say, "Can't I get a minute's peace around here?" instead of "I really need some time to rest. Can I play with you after dinner?"

Deletions are constructed in three ways:

- **Statements in the form of a question.** Statement: "Can't you be quiet for just a minute?" (Translation: "I'd really like to see the end of this show.")

- **Requests in the form of neutral observations.** Statement: "Karen really liked that new movie." (Translation: "Let's go see that new movie.")

- **Deleted references that exclude important information.** Statement: "There's been a lot of tension in this house lately." (Translation: "I've been angry with you ever since you embarrassed me at that party.")

Substitution

Through substitution, family members express their feelings, but in a safer way or with a safer person. If a son is taught that "boys don't cry," he might rechannel his hurt into anger. If a wife is unhappy at work but doesn't feel comfortable criticizing her boss, she might come home and yell at her husband for spending too much time at the golf course.

Incongruent Messages

As you learned in Chapter Four, incongruent messages occur when the signals sent by your nonverbals don't match what you are saying. A wife tells her husband, "Don't worry about it — we can do without those things," after he forgets to go to the grocery, but she says it in a harsh, angry tone with her teeth clenched. When individuals use incongruent messages, the rest of their family is forced to guess at their real meaning. Often, this doesn't work and tensions only increase.

Covert Manipulation Strategies

When families have communication disorders like those described above, individuals do not feel free to make requests. Instead, family members must resort to manipulation to get what they want. The following eight manipulation strategies are common in families that cannot communicate openly (McKay, Davis, and Fanning 226-28):

Blaming and Judging

Blamers attack the other members of their family for not meeting their needs. They often hit below the belt, attacking sensitive areas of their family members' self-esteem. Because this strategy creates fear, it can be successful for a short time. Eventually, however, the other members of the family become immune to the blamer's rants and accusations.

Playing on Guilt

Subtly, some people let their families know that they are in pain. They are the essence of incongruence, saying they are fine while looking miserable, sighing a lot, and reminding family members of past sins. Family members do things for this individual, not because they want to, but because they feel they should.

Seeking Pity

This individual acts helpless and pathetic, playing the victim. Family members help these people because they feel sorry for them. Like the use of blame, this technique wears thin quickly, becoming less effective the more it is used.

Blackmail

Blackmailers threaten other family members in order to get their way. They may do it in an overt or a covert way, but they let family members know there will be no dinner, no trip to the park, no new skateboard, or even no sex unless they get their way. In the extreme, some blackmailers even threaten to leave the family if their demands aren't met.

Bribery

Bribers use flattery, attention, favors, and presents to get their way. Parents may tell a child that he will get that special toy if he behaves at the restaurant; a husband may bring his wife breakfast in bed when he wants something from her.

Placating

Avoiding conflict and acting sacrificially within the family structure, placaters hope that they will motivate others to do things for them in return. They operate on the belief, "I've been so nice to you, you should be nice to me." The problem with this technique is that other family members often take placaters for granted and are unaware of their needs. Consequently, individuals who placate often become long-suffering martyrs with hidden resentments.

Turning Cold

One of the most dangerous and hurtful manipulation strategies is to withhold love from family members, replacing it with chilly silence and emotional withdrawal. This technique is particularly effective with children since they depend so heavily on their parent's love. However, turning cold can cause deep-seated resentment and rage.

Developing Symptoms

Already discussed in Chapter Five as a way to avoid conflict, family members may also develop symptoms to indirectly express their needs. If children don't get enough attention from their parents, for example, they may get into trouble at school. Obviously, all of these manipulation strategies are a result of families who cannot communicate openly with each other. People who use these techniques may be successful in getting what they want, but they will create greater problems in the process. Therefore, these strategies should be avoided at all costs and replaced with healthier and more productive techniques.

Skills for Healthy Family Communication

To communicate more productively in your family, and to improve your family relationships, strive for the following:

Reasonable Expectations

When first married, newlyweds sometimes believe their marriage will be perfect. When life intervenes and the inevitable stress and conflict arise, these couples are often disappointed. If you have unrealistic expectations for your marriage or family, you will be dissatisfied with any existing relationship.

Self-Disclosure

As in all communication situations, it is necessary for family members to reveal their thoughts, feelings, concerns, and desires to each other. Remember that self-disclosure breeds self-disclosure. If a parent is honest with a child, the child will behave in kind. If a husband discusses his feelings, his wife will feel more comfortable revealing hers. When you disclose, be sure to keep the focus on your feelings, not past wrongs, and use the principles of assertive communication.

Empathic Understanding

When couples and families seek counseling, they are often asked to participate in role-playing exercises and discuss issues from the other person's point of view. The reason for this is that empathy — the ability to see the world from another person's perspective and to feel what that person feels — is an important element in any relationship. Try to see the world, and your family, from the perspective of your family members. It can help you to listen carefully when they disclose and to ask questions seeking information.

Openness to Change

Being responsive requires more than understanding the members of your family. You must also work to meet their needs, which often requires change. Further, if your family practices manipulation strategies or harmful communication patterns, you must be willing to replace those habits (which can be well ingrained) with healthier communication strategies.

Fair Fighting

Because most problems in families occur when there is conflict, effective family communication begins with productive conflict management. Apply the principles from Chapter Five regarding fair fighting. Remember to accept and confirm others while asserting yourself, respect diversity, create a supportive climate for conflict management, show grace, find a good time and a private location for your fight, define the specific issues being debated, be prepared, withhold quick retorts, and fight about issues that you can solve.

Qualities and Characteristics of Effective Parents

You may or may not be a parent now, but chances are that you will be at some point. Approximately 85 percent of people become parents during their lifetime. This, and the fact that parents are most responsible for the communication patterns used in a family, necessitates a look at parent effectiveness. What does it take to be a good parent? How can you raise children who are moral, ethical, and responsible? Unfortunately, there is no definitive answer to those questions. There are, however, steps that can be taken by parents to promote healthy communication in their homes.

Listening

Family therapist Stephanie Martson says, "Every family should extend First Amendment rights to all its members, but this freedom is particularly essential for our kids. Children must be able to say what they think, openly express their feelings, and ask for what they want and need if they are ever able to develop an integrated sense of self." When you listen to children, remember the following:

- **Focus your attention on your child.** It is very easy to pretend to listen to a child while watching TV, reading, or working. You can show your children that you really care about what they say by putting everything else away, making eye contact, and making sure you aren't distracted as you listen.

- **Listen to both words and feelings.** If necessary, ask questions to ensure that you know what the child feels.

- **Don't always try to solve a child's problems.** Sometimes kids just need to know that they have been heard. However, as adults, we have a tendency to lecture children and attempt to solve all their problems for them. While there is a time and a place for teaching, there is also a time and a place for listening.

Expressing

Expressing yourself clearly is just as important with children as with adults. Strive for the following:

- **Specificity.** Tell children exactly what is expected of them. How can they behave if they don't know what you want?

- **Immediacy.** Studies show that children learn best when they receive rewards or discipline immediately following their behavior.

- **Non-Judgment.** When disciplining children, always focus on the behavior and not the child. If you tell children they are "bad," they will believe you.

- **Self-Disclosure.** Revealing a little of yourself can make you seem more human and less of an authority figure to your children.

- **Congruency.** Because children have less experience

interpreting nonverbals, they can be especially confused by nonverbal signals that don't match the verbal message.

Joint Problem Solving

A cooperative approach to problem solving helps prevent parents from being too authoritarian or too permissive and gives children ownership over the solution chosen. There are six steps in joint problem solving: identifying and defining the conflict, generating possible solutions, evaluating the proposed solutions, choosing the best one, implementing the decision, and evaluating the results.

Discipline

Children want and need discipline. According to the National PTA, discipline is needed for the protection of children, to help them get along with others, and to teach them limits. Discipline helps children learn values, ethics, and morals, teaches them to think and act in an orderly manner, and helps them understand that their behavior has consequences. Dr. Ray Guarendi, clinical psychologist, speaker, and author, explains why discipline must begin with parents. "The prime motive for discipline," he notes, "is this: you are the kindest, gentlest teacher that your children will ever have. Never again will they be taught how to get along in life with a fraction of your love." But disciplining isn't easy, so here are some suggestions to help you discipline children effectively:

- **Be consistent.** Dr. Guarendi defines consistency as "reacting similarly to a recurrent behavior." When a child does something, you must respond in a predictable way. Eighty percent consistency is desirable, but most parents hover between 20 and 40 percent. This means if you tell a child to pick up her toys three times before she acts, your consistency is at 33 percent. Consistency is important because it takes the guesswork out of discipline (for both the parent and the child) and actually leads to less discipline. That is, the more consistent parents are, the less children misbehave.

- **Don't impose too many rules.** Before making a rule, ask the following questions: Is the rule age-appropriate? Does it protect the health and safety of the child? Does it protect the rights or property of others?

- **Keep rules simple and understandable.** Children will follow rules if they understand the reason behind them. For instance, a four-year-old needs to know he is not allowed to cross the street alone because he could be hurt.

- **Offer praise for good behavior and accomplishments.** Children are more likely to repeat a positive behavior for which they receive praise than avoid a negative behavior for which they are punished.

- **Discipline from a position of love.** When children misbehave, let them know you disapprove of their behavior, not them. Always tell your children that you love them when disciplining them.

- **Be a good role model.** Your behavior will have far more impact than any rule or punishment given to children. They learn to behave by watching and imitating adults, especially their parents. "Do as I say, not as I do" simply does not work.

Developing Self-Esteem in Children

Self-esteem, or the amount of satisfaction you have with yourself, is very important to children. Children with high self-esteem are better able to handle conflicts, take responsibility, and resist negative pressures. They are more optimistic and enjoy life. Children who do not feel good about themselves become frustrated and anxious when faced with challenges, avoid trying new things, and are more easily influenced. They may become passive, withdrawn, and depressed.

Since parents, more than anyone else, influence a child's self-esteem, here are some suggestions to ensure that influence is positive:

- **Be generous with praise.** It is not enough merely to offer general praise like, "You're a good girl." You must be specific

145

and use what is called descriptive praise. If your child completes a chore, you could say, "You did a great job of setting the table. You put everything in the right place and made it look so nice for dinner." If your child has a special talent, say, "You have a wonderful singing voice. Your range is remarkably broad." But you need to be truthful with your praise or it will lose its impact. If your child doesn't make the basketball team, don't say, "Next time you'll make the team and be the star!" Instead, praise the child for what he did do well. You could say, "I'm really proud of the effort you gave."

- **Redirect your child's inaccurate beliefs.** "The pervasive step for parents to take is to identify kids' irrational beliefs about themselves," says pediatric psychologist Brian Messinger, Ph.D. "Whether they are about perfection, attractiveness, ability, or anything else, these inaccurate perceptions can take root and become reality to a child" ("Developing Your Child's ... "). For instance, a child may say, "I can't do math. I'm no good at school." This is an inaccurate overgeneralization. Reframe the situation for the child by saying, "You are a good student. I'm very happy with your grades. You just need to work a little harder on math. I'll help you."

- **Give children love and affection.** Hugs, kisses, and physical contact make a child feel valued and important.

- **Give positive, accurate feedback.** Telling a child, "You'd lose your head if it wasn't attached," makes a child feel that he is not only absent-minded, but that he has no control over it. Instead, tell a child what they do and how to fix the problem. For instance, you could say, "You don't always put your things away in the proper spot. I think you would lose things less often if you were more organized."

- **Teach your children to practice positive self-talk.** What we think determines how we feel and how we behave. In fact, research has found that negative self-talk causes depression and anxiety. Therefore, it is important for parents to teach

146

children how to talk to themselves. At four, my son became very nervous about new situations after he broke his leg. Being transported, going to the doctor, and facing surgery caused him great anxiety. To help himself through these situations, he would repeat the mantra, "Please be brave, Quinn," over and over until he felt comfortable again.

- **Create a safe, nurturing home environment.** Children who do not feel safe or who are abused tend to have very low self-esteem. In your home, children should feel protected physically and emotionally.

Conclusion

Though families are as diverse as the people in them, one fact remains constant: no other relationship will have as much impact on you as the relationship you have with your family. Avoiding unhealthy and manipulative behavior while engaging in productive, healthy communication with your family can vastly improve the quality of life for you and your loved ones.

Chapter Nine

Intercultural Communication

Communicating across cultures presents special difficulties. Because people from different cultures have different attitudes, beliefs, and experiences, misunderstandings can easily occur when they interact. Numerous companies have learned that when advertising in foreign countries, slogans that work in America often aren't as effective. Consider the following examples:

- Coors translated its slogan, "Turn It Loose," into Spanish, where it was read as "Suffer from Diarrhea."

- Frank Purdue's trademark line, "It takes a tough man to make a tender chicken," didn't have quite the same meaning in Spanish. Translated, the slogan became, "It takes a sexually stimulated man to make a chicken affectionate."

- At Chevrolet, no one could understand why the Nova didn't sell well in Spanish-speaking countries until it was explained to them that "no va" means "it doesn't go" in Spanish.

- Puffs tissues had a similar problem in Germany, where "Puff" is slang for a whorehouse.

- The slogan, "Pepsi Brings You Back to Life," was translated much too literally in China. Prospective consumers there were promised, "Pepsi Brings Your Ancestors Back from the Grave."

- After introducing the "Mist Stick" in Germany, Clairol learned that "mist" is slang for manure. Not too many people had use for the "Manure Stick."

- When Gerber first started selling baby food in Africa, they used the same packaging as in the United States, with a cute baby on the label. Later, they discovered that since so many people in Africa can't read, companies routinely put pictures on the label of what's inside the package.

Chances are, any misunderstanding you encounter when you communicate with individuals from other cultures will not be as embarrassing or costly as the mistakes made by these companies. But, as technology increases and our world becomes smaller, it becomes more important for all of us to learn to communicate with diverse groups of people. Doing so cannot only help us professionally, it can also be extremely rewarding.

What Is Culture?

Culture is our way of life. It includes the ideas, values, beliefs, customs, language, and behavior patterns that are handed down from one generation to another. Intercultural communication, then, is communication that occurs between people with different cultural beliefs, or ways of behaving. The study of this aspect of communication has grown rapidly in the past few years as our world has become more globalized and as society has placed a greater emphasis on diversity and multiculturalism.

To better understand what culture is and how it affects our communication patterns, it is helpful to understand its attributes. In the book *Thinking Through Communication*, Sarah Trenholm identifies the following basic characteristics of culture (314-19):

Cultures Are Learned

We are not born with any cultural predispositions. Instead, we behave like others in our culture because we are taught to do so. In fact, we are so indoctrinated into our culture that our cultural norms appear to be natural and right and we can't imagine acting or thinking differently. If you had been born in Japan to Japanese parents, however, you would speak Japanese, follow Japanese customs, and see the world from an Asian point of view.

Cultures Are Shared

A culture reflects the beliefs and behaviors of a large group of people. Therefore, within our culture we feel bound to meet the norms and expectations of others and we spend a great deal of time and energy trying to do so.

Cultures Are Multi-Faceted

Culture is a very complex concept and affects many aspects of our lives. Says Trenholm, "At a minimum, culture affects language, religion, basic worldview, education, social organization, technology, politics, and law, and all of these factors affect one another" (318).

Cultures Are Dynamic

As the world changes, so do cultures. Though the changes are sometimes gradual, we must continually learn new rules and norms to behave properly in our culture. In America, for instance, increased awareness of the danger of second-hand smoke has greatly affected how we view smoking. Fifty years ago, it would not have been at all unusual for someone to light a cigarette in a public place such as a movie theatre. Today, smoking is almost always banned in such locations and some communities have gone so far as to make smoking in any public place illegal. Because of the dynamic nature of culture, you cannot hope to assimilate into a new culture by memorizing a list of dos and don'ts. Instead, you must remain flexible and sensitive to the behavior of others.

Cultural Identities Overlap

Each one of us belongs to a variety of overlapping cultures, some of which work together and some of which conflict. You may simultaneously have a national culture, an ethnic culture, a family culture, a religious culture, an age culture, and a gender culture. This makes each of us unique, even within one culture, but can also create internal conflicts when our different identities clash. For example, your nationalism may motivate you to serve in the military, but your religion causes you to be opposed to killing.

Why Communicate Across Cultures?

We live in a world that is becoming more and more interdependent. Global problems, such as pollution, the depletion of the ozone, and terrorism cannot be solved by one nation. Instead, people all across the globe must work together to find solutions. Technology has also linked cultures in ways previously unheard of. Years ago, we were very isolated from people in different parts of the world. Today, we can travel across oceans and continents in a matter of hours, or communicate with anyone in the world instantaneously via phone or the Internet. We can even watch distant events live through satellite technology. During the world wars, people had to wait days for news from the front. Now, people watch historical events as they happen on television. Thus, it has become almost impossible for any one nation or culture to isolate itself from the rest of the world, making intercultural communication a necessity. We must learn to communicate across cultures for the following reasons:

We Live in a Global Village

Mass media and the technology mentioned above (telephones, television, radio, and the Internet) make events that take place anywhere immediately known to people everywhere. When the Berlin Wall fell, people around the world watched it being torn down by jubilant Germans. If there is a terrorist strike in Israel, a housewife in Wyoming will be shown the aftermath and hear the comments of witnesses only moments after the strike. Further, transportation technology allows you to wake up in Africa and go to bed in North America. In short, intercultural contact, whether direct or vicarious, is fairly common in today's world. Media writer Marshall McLuhan called this phenomenon "the global village" (Zeuschner 386) and, like it or not, we are all residents. Therefore, we must learn how to communicate with our fellow "villagers."

We Have a Global Economy

Not only do we interact with people from other parts of the world, so does our money. If you have ever traveled to another country, you may have been surprised to see so many American products. When in London, I encountered McDonalds, Burger King, Taco Bell, Pizza Hut, and Dunkin' Donuts all within one square mile! Likewise, we use foreign goods and labor extensively. Conflict in the Middle East has the potential to curtail our oil supplies. A recession in Asia can affect the United States stock market. Therefore, we are linked to different cultures in one of the most fundamental ways: our pocketbooks.

We Have Many Cultures in Our Own Neighborhoods

We don't have to travel to foreign countries to encounter a different culture. America is a land of diverse peoples and numerous sub-cultures. In order to get along with our neighbors who have different cultural backgrounds, we must be able to communicate with them.

Intercultural Communication Is Especially Rewarding

When we interact with people from different cultures, we broaden our knowledge and experience, learn to understand people with vastly different experiences, and have the opportunity to view the world from a different perspective. As a teacher, some of my most meaningful relationships have been with exchange students from countries as diverse as Russia, Germany, and Paraguay.

How Culture Affects Communication

If all people in all cultures communicated the same way, there would be no need to study intercultural communication. The problem is, that simply doesn't happen. Your culture significantly affects the way you communicate, often in such deeply-rooted ways that you don't even realize it. Culture affects patterns and habits of communication in the following ways (Trenholm, 323-28):

Culture Affects Our Perception

Culture is a filter through which we view people, behavior, and events. Because of this, people from two different cultures may perceive the exact same event completely differently. Trenholm tells the story of an American engineering company who spent months negotiating a huge contract with a Saudi Arabian firm (323-24). When the two sides had reached an agreement, the American company bound the contract in an expensive pigskin portfolio. The Saudis, however, consider the pig an unclean animal and interpreted what was supposed to be a goodwill gesture as a terrible insult. The Saudi firm burned the proposal and the contract and threw the Americans out of their country. In this case, a costly misunderstanding was the result of the exact same event being interpreted in two completely different ways.

Culture Affects Our Role Identities

A second way culture affects communication is by dictating how we should behave according to our age, gender, status, occupation, or class. In some parts of the world, women are expected to behave in a much more subservient manner than in western countries. Some countries show their elders great respect while Americans value youth and see old age as a time of diminished capacity.

Culture Affects Our Goals

Our culture tells us what goals and aspirations we should pursue. Many Americans work hard to acquire status symbols such as luxury automobiles, expensive homes, designer clothing, and top-of-the-line electronic equipment. Many people in other cultures would not understand spending so much money on such items.

Culture Affects Our Images of Ourselves

Our culture affects our sense of self and, consequently, our interactions with others. For instance, some cultures (including America) teach that individualism is more valuable while other cultures emphasize collectivism, or the belief that individual rights and goals should be sacrificed for the good of others. Such beliefs are reflected even in the way people in such cultures say names. In America, the individual name always comes first while in China, the family name is stated before the personal name.

Barriers to Intercultural Understanding

The first step in repairing a problem is to identify it. If you go to the doctor, he must diagnose the cause of your illness before he can treat it. When you visit your mechanic, he will first find the cause of that funny noise your car is making before he begins to fix it. Likewise, before we can improve our skills in intercultural communication, we must identify the barriers that make this form of communication so difficult.

Stereotypes and Prejudices

Stereotypes are generalizations we make about types within a category. For instance, we believe that large cities have more crime and traffic than smaller towns. Or, when applied to people, that the French are great lovers. Or that the Japanese are all workaholics. Stereotypes serve a function in that they help reduce our anxiety when we confront a new situation. If we believe that this experience will be similar to a past experience, it will cause us to be less nervous. I may think, "My new coworker is from Russia. I bet he'll be like Alex, another Russian who used to work here." The danger with stereotypes is that, since they are overgeneralized, they are often inaccurate. Also, the danger exists that stereotypes can turn into prejudices, which are negative stereotypes that individuals or groups hold toward members of another group. Obviously, when we hold prejudices toward members of another culture, we are not prepared to communicate with them in a positive way.

Ethnocentrism

If you believe that your culture is superior to any other, you are practicing ethnocentrism. Of course, there is nothing wrong with taking pride in your heritage. Ethnocentrism goes beyond that to the feeling that you know better and even are better than others simply because they are from a different culture. When I traveled through Europe with a group of Americans, I heard many ethnocentric comments. Some of my fellow travelers would refer to our hosts as "backwards" or talk about how some countries "had not yet caught up to America." Again, it is difficult to communicate with someone on an equal basis if you do not perceive them as equal.

Assumed Similarity

When we assume similarity, we forget that there actually are differences between members of different cultures in terms of goals, motives, values, and perception and act on the belief that "everyone is essentially the same under the skin." We cannot understand, appreciate, and accommodate differences if we do not believe they exist.

Filters and Screens

Filters and screens are psychological barriers to listening that we use to allow ourselves to hear only what we want to hear. These mechanisms are often the result of our values, experiences, fears, and expectations. You've probably known someone who had a

155

"block" when it came to certain information. No matter how many times he was told something, he refused to hear or believe. For instance, your grandfather may not be the driver he once was. His reactions aren't as quick, his judgment is not as sharp, and his habit of driving slowly in the passing lane is annoying, if not dangerous. However, whenever anyone suggests that he let others take him places, he refuses to listen. His ego and his desire for independence cause him to filter any information that he does not really want to know. When communicating with someone from a different culture, filters and screens become much more intense.

Anxiety and Avoidance

Because intercultural communication is often an unfamiliar situation, it causes stress and anxiety. When these emotions become too great, individuals may choose to simply avoid communicating with people from cultures other than their own.

Offensive Behavior

In Chapter Four, we discussed how the first President Bush offended the Australians by showing what he thought was the peace sign. He didn't realize that he had his hand turned the wrong way, forming what is considered an obscene gesture in Australia. In Arabian cultures, the left hand is considered "unclean" because it is reserved for toilet procedures. If an American visiting an Arabian country were to eat with his left hand (which would be perfectly normal within his own culture), he would cause his hosts great offense. The fact that we can do something that is completely normal in our culture and offend someone in another culture is another barrier to cultural understanding.

Culture Shock

A special problem with intercultural communication that occurs when an individual enters a foreign culture is culture shock. Though it is a normal reaction to situations that are very new and different, like traveling to a new country, joining the military, or going away to college, it can be a very traumatic and frustrating experience. Anthropologist Kalvero Oberg, who coined the term, describes four stages of culture shock (177-182):

Stage One: The Honeymoon

When you first enter a new culture, the experience is very exciting. A newly married couple enjoys the novelty and romance of their new relationship. Someone who moves to a foreign country will, at first, be enamored with the new sights, people, and experiences. Tourists often don't stay in one place long enough for this stage to wear off.

Stage Two: The Crisis

This is the "shock" in "culture shock." When the excitement of a new experience wears off, the day-to-day realities set in and the differences between your own culture and the new one create problems. In a marriage, you start to notice the annoying habits of your partner. The individual who has moved to a new country may find it difficult to learn the language and may realize that even the simplest tasks, like ordering from a menu in a restaurant, create problems. In one study of students studying abroad, it was found that 25 percent of the students experienced depression during their stay in another country. So, if you experience culture shock, remember that your feelings are not unique. Also remember that if you deal with your problems and stick with the experience, you will move to ...

Stage Three: Recovery

During this phase, you gain the skills necessary to function effectively in your new environment. The married couple learns to compromise; the person living in a new country starts to learn the language and becomes acclimated to the customs of his new home.

Stage Four: Adjustment

In adjustment, you function so well in your new environment that it almost seems automatic. The married couple becomes so interdependent they can no longer imagine life on their own; the foreigner becomes so acclimated to everyday life in his new country he doesn't have to search for translations or think about converting currency.

How to Communicate Across Cultures

So now that we know that intercultural communication is unavoidable, difficult, and not without barriers, the question becomes how do we do it? How can we communicate with people from cultures vastly different from our own without causing gross misunderstandings or offending them? If you have questions like these, you're in luck because here are the answers.

Open Yourself to Intercultural Communication

Don't let your anxieties or the inherent difficulties of communicating across cultures keep you from meeting others who may be different from you. Avoiding intercultural communication may keep you from some of the most rewarding interpersonal relationships you will ever have.

Prepare Yourself

The best way to prepare yourself to communicate with someone from another culture is to learn about that culture. Talk to others from that culture, read about it, or maybe take a class on the language or history of the culture you will encounter. If you plan to live with or do business with members of another culture, this is an absolutely essential step.

Acknowledge and Face Your Fears

Don't deny that you are anxious before you engage in intercultural communication. Acknowledge your nervousness and then deal with it. If you are worried that you won't be accepted by a group, evaluate that fear honestly. Is it realistic? What are the consequences if it happens? What can you do to prevent it from happening? Most likely, if you examine a fear rationally, you will see that it is groundless.

Recognize Differences

Don't assume similarities. When interacting with diverse individuals, expect differences between yourself and those you encounter and also between individual members of that group. No two people are alike, even when they share the same culture.

Recognize Your Prejudices and Stereotypes

You will never overcome the barrier that prejudices and stereotypes present unless you admit that you have them. Acknowledge that you may hold unfair attitudes toward others, then work to move past those beliefs.

Engage in Person-Centered Communication

When you communicate with others from diverse cultures, try to understand their point of view and take it into account. For instance, Julia T. Wood recommends avoiding slang terms and idioms when speaking to someone from another country (159). Though the individual may speak English very well, such language is often uniquely American and would not be recognized by someone who learned English as a foreign language.

Respect Others' Feelings and Ideas

A good communicator never, in any circumstance, denies or diminishes the feelings of another. This is especially true in intercultural communication. When communicating with people from other cultures we must remember that they may respond differently to situations than we would because different cultural backgrounds give individuals different ways of thinking, feeling, and emoting.

Don't Fall Prey to Ethnocentrism

Remember that standards of normality, correctness, and even morality vary among cultures. You don't necessarily have to agree with everything someone from a different culture says or does, but you can acknowledge that they are making their decisions from within the framework of a cultural context different from your own.

Follow Cultural Rules and Customs

If you find yourself in a different culture, abide by the rules of that culture, even when those rules seem odd to you. In some Asian cultures, it is expected that guests take their shoes off before entering someone else's home. If you visit such a country, follow this custom. Otherwise, you run the risk of causing your hosts great offense.

Practice Intercultural Communication

Learning to competently respond to diversity is a process that takes time. Therefore, you should seek out any opportunity you have to practice such skills. Interact with a larger circle of acquaintances. Travel. Host an exchange student. Take part in conferences and workshops that bring people together from all across the world. The more you interact with people from other cultures, the better you'll be at doing so.

Conclusion

Many of the most memorable and rewarding interpersonal relationships I have enjoyed have been with people vastly different from myself. Though there are difficulties to overcome, intercultural communication is an experience that is well worth the effort. Now that you understand the barriers to intercultural communication and know guidelines for interacting with diverse individuals, you can better discover the joy of communicating with people from cultures different from your own.

Bibliography

Adler, Mortimer J. *How to Speak. How to Listen.* New York: MacMillan, 1983.

Bettinghaus, Erwin P. and Michael J. Cody. *Persuasive Communication.* 4th ed. New York: Holt, Rinehart, and Winston, Inc., 1987.

Booher, Dianna. *Communicate with Confidence.* New York: McGraw-Hill Trade, Inc., 1994.

Borchers, Tim. "Interpersonal Conflict." (http://www.abacon.com/commstudies/interpersonal/inconflict.html). 1999.

Briggs, Bill. "Body Language." *The Denver Post.* March 20, 2001: E-1.

Bush, George W. "President George W. Bush's Inaugural Address." (http://www.whitehouse.gov/news/inaugural-address.html). January 20, 2001.

CNN with Ann Humphries "Selling Yourself Again: The Job Interview Revisited." (http://www.cnn.com/2001/CAREER/corporateclass/04/19/interviewee/index.html). April 19, 2001.

Canter, Lee and Marlene. *Parents On Your Side.* Santa Monica, CA: Lee Canter & Associates, 1991.

Crowley, Geoffrey with Mary Hager and Adam Rogers. "Dialing the Stress-Meter Down." *Newsweek.* March 6, 1995: 62.

De Pree, Max. *Leadership Is an Art.* New York: Doubleday, 1989.

"Developing Your Child's Self-Esteem." Updated and reviewed by Kim Rutherford, M.D. (http://www.kidshealth.org/parent/emotions/feelings/self_esteem.html). September, 2001.

DeVito, Joseph A. *Human Communication: The Basic Course.* 7th ed. New York: Addison-Wesley Publishing Company, 1997.

"Discipline: A Parent's Guide." The National PTA. (http://npin.org/library/pre1998/n00203/n00203.html), 1993.

Dornin, Rusty. "Shyness Is Increasing in a Less Social World." (http://www.cnn.com/HEALTH/9510/shyness/index.html). October 16, 1995.

Dowling, Tim. "When Words Collide." *Men's Health.* May, 1996: 60-61.

Emmert, Philip and William C. Donaghy. *Human Communication: Elements and Contexts.* Reading, MA: Addison-Wesley Publishing Company, Inc., 1981.

Franklin, Sharon and Deborah J. Clark. *Nextext Essentials of Speech Communication.* Evanston, IL: McDougal Littell, 2001.

"Fung Shui? What's Fung Shui?" (http://hometownone.com/articles/fung_shui.asp).

Gallagher, Julie. "On the Verge of Voice Commerce." (http://www.insurancetech.com/it2/story/specialReport/IST20 010308S0008). March 8, 2001.

Gronbeck, Bruce E., Kathleen German, Douglas Ehninger, and Alan H. Monroe. *Principles of Speech Communication.* 13th Brief ed. New York: Addison-Wesley Educational Publishers Inc., 1998.

Guarendi, Ray. "The Importance of Discipline: Who Will Discipline Your Children, If Not You?" (http://family.go.com/raisingkids/child/behavior/feature/maho78ray/maho78ray.html).

Guarendi, Ray. "Striving for Consistent Discipline: Consistency is Indispensable to Competent Parenting." (http://family.go.com/raisingkids/child/skills/feature/maho47ray/maho47ray.html).

Hackman, Michael Z. and Craig E. Johnson. *Leadership: A Communication Perspective.* Prospect Heights, IL: Waveland Press, Inc., 1991.

"Helping Your Child Develop Self-Esteem." (http://www.childdevelopmentinfo.com/parenting.self_esteem. sthml). Child Development Institute, 2000.

Infante, Dominic A., Andrew S. Rancer, and Deanna F. Womack. *Building Communication Theory*. Prospect Heights, IL: Waveland Press, Inc., 1990.

Jaasma, Marjorie A. "Classroom Communication Apprehension: Does Being Male or Female Make a Difference?" *Communication Reports*. Volume 10, No. 2, Summer, 1997: 219-228.

Kendall, Bridget. "Getting to Know You." (http://news.bbc.co.uk/hi/ english/world/from_our_own_correspondent/newsid_1392000 /1392170.stm). June 16, 2001.

Littlejohn, Stephen. *Theories of Human Communication*. 2nd ed. Belmont, CA: Wadsworth Publishing Company, 1983.

"Low Marriage, High Divorce Rate Hits Kids Hard." Reuters. (http://www.vix.com/men/nofather/articles/usa-marriage.html). April 4, 1995.

Luft, Joseph. *Of Human Interaction*. Palo Alto, CA: Mayfield Publishing Company, 1969.

Marrs, Carol. *The Complete Book of Speech Communication*. Colorado Springs, CO: Meriwether Publishing, Ltd., 1992.

"Master Debaters." (http://www.historyhouse.com/uts/presidential _debates). October 1, 2000.

Mathews, Jay. "The Shrinking Field." (http://washingtonpost.com/ wp-srv/politics/campaigns/wh2000/stories/tall080399.htm). August 3, 1999.

Matusak, Larraine R. *Finding Your Voice: Learning to Lead ... Anywhere You Want to Make a Difference*. San Francisco: Jossey-Bass Publishers, 1996.

McCutcheon, Randall, James Schaffer, and Joseph R. Wycoff. *Communication Matters*. St. Paul, MN: Glencoe McGraw Hill, 1994.

McKay, Matthew, Ph.D., Martha Davis, Ph.D., and Patrick Fanning. *Messages: The Communication Skills Book.* Oakland, CA: New Harbinger Publications, 1983.

Molloy, John T. *Molloy's Live for Success.* New York: Bantam Books, 1981.

Morris, Desmond. *With Words Unspoken: The Nonverbal Experience.* New York: Holt, Rinehart & Winston, 1976.

Norton, Robert. *Communicator Style: Theory, Applications, and Measures.* Beverly Hills, CA: Sage Publications, 1983.

O'Connor, J. Regis. *Speech: Exploring Communication.* 4th ed. Lincolnweed, IL: National Textbook Company, 1996.

O'Donnell, Olive M. "Parents Helping Parents: A Guide for Action." (http://www.parentingisprevention.org/pipp_booklet/index.html). March, 1999.

Oberg, Kalvero. "Culture Shock: Adjustment to New Cultural Environments." *Practical Anthropology 7,* 1960.

Pryce, Delina D. and Jonas Voss.
"Don't Shy Away. Tackle This Quiz Head-On." (http://www.usnews.com/usnews/nycu/health/shyqz.htm).

Qubein, Nido R. *How to Be a Great Communicator: In Person, on Paper, and on the Podium.* New York: John Wiley & Sons, Inc., 1996.

Richmond, Virginia P. and James C. McCroskey. *Nonverbal Behavior in Interpersonal Relations.* 4th ed. Needham Heights, MA: Allyn & Bacon, 1999.

Ruberman, T.R. "Psychosocial Influences on Mortality of Patients with Coronary Heart Disease." *Journal of the American Medical Association, 267.* January 22-29, 1992: 559-560.

Ryan, Robin. "A New Interviewing Approach." (http://www.cnn.com/2000/CAREER/careercenter/06/20/intvu.tech.wc/index.html). June 20, 2000.

Schrof, Joannie M. and Stacey Schultz. "For Millions of Americans, Every Day Is a Struggle With Debilitating Shyness." *U.S. News & World Report.* June 21, 1999.

Stadter, Mike. "Managing Interpersonal Conflict by Paying Attention to Interests: Yours and Theirs." (http://www.business-mediation.com/news_mpr199004b.html). April, 1990.

Sutter, Lorie M. "Birth Order." (http://ohioline.osu.edu/hyg-fact/5000/5279.html).

Trenholm, Sarah. *Thinking Through Communication: An Introduction to the Study of Human Communication.* Needham Heights, MA: Allyn G. Bacon, 1995.

Van Ekeren, Glenn. *Speakers Sourcebook II: Quotes, Stories & Anecdotes for Every Occasion.* Paramus, NJ: Prentice-Hall, Inc., 1994.

Wesson, Nancy, Ph.D. "Overcoming Shyness." (http://www.wespsych.com/shyness.html#anxiety).

Williams, Jane L. *Discipline That Works.* Washington, DC: National Education Association of the United States, Stock No. 5165-3, 1987. (http://www.nea.org/parents/tools/disc.html).

Wood, Julia T. *Communication Mosaics: An Introduction to the Field of Communication.* 2nd ed. Belmont, CA: Wadsworth Publishing Company, 2000.

Work, William. "On Communication Apprehension: Everything You've Wanted to Know But Have Been Afraid to Ask." *Communication Education.* July, 1982.

Wu, Shelley, Ph.D. "Color Psychology: Meanings and Effects of Color." (http://psychology.about.com/library/bl/blcolor_pink1.htm).

Zeuschner, Raymond. *Communicating Today.* 2nd ed. Needham Heights, MA: Allyn & Bacon, 1996.

NOTE: The information in this bibliography was correct at the time of printing.

About the Author

Brent Oberg teaches communication, speech, and television production at Highlands Ranch High School in Highlands Ranch, Colorado, a suburb of Denver. In his role as coach of the Highlands Ranch Speech and Debate Team, Brent has seen his students qualify for finals, semi-finals, and quarterfinals at the national tournament and win numerous state and tournament championships. He has also coached a national champion in the National Management Association Oratorical Contest, a national runner-up in the American Legion Oratorical Contest, and a national finalist in the VFW Voice of Democracy Contest. He has taught speech and coached forensics at the junior high, high school, and university levels.

Brent holds a bachelor's degree in speech and English education from the University of Wyoming and a master's degree in communication from Regis University in Denver.

Also the author of *Speechcraft: An Introduction to Public Speaking* and *Forensics: The Winner's Guide to Speech Contests*, Brent lives in Highlands Ranch with his wife, Beth, and his children Quinn, Soren, and Zoe. He loves to travel, hike, golf, and, more than anything else, spend time with his family.

Order Form

Meriwether Publishing Ltd.
PO Box 7710
Colorado Springs CO 80933-7710
Phone: 800-937-5297 Fax: 719-594-9916
Website: www.meriwether.com

Please send me the following books:

_____ **Interpersonal Communication #BK-B260** **$16.95**
by Brent C. Oberg
An introduction to human interaction

_____ **Forensics #BK-B179** **$16.95**
by Brent C. Oberg
The winner's guide to speech contests

_____ **Speechcraft #BK-B149** **$16.95**
by Brent C. Oberg
An introduction to public speaking

_____ **The Complete Book of Speech** **$14.95**
Communication #BK-B142
by Carol Marrs
Ideas and activities for speech and theatre

_____ **Two Character Plays for Student Actors** **$16.95**
#BK-B174
by Robert Mauro
A collection of 15 one-act plays

_____ **Theatre Games and Beyond #BK-B217** **$16.95**
by Amiel Schotz
A creative approach for performers

_____ **Theatre Games for Young Performers #BK-B188** **$16.95**
by Maria C. Novelly
Improvisations and exercises for developing acting skills

These and other fine Meriwether Publishing books are available at
your local bookstore or direct from the publisher. Prices subject to
change without notice. Check our website or call for current prices.

Name: _____ e-mail: _____

Organization name: _____

Address: _____

City: _____ State: _____

Zip: _____ Phone: _____

❑ **Check enclosed**

❑ **Visa / MasterCard / Discover #** _____

Signature: _____ Expiration
date: _____
(required for credit card orders)

Colorado residents: Please add 3% sales tax.
Shipping: Include $4.95 for the first book and 75¢ for each additional book ordered.

❑ *Please send me a copy of your complete catalog of books and plays.*